PRISM OF SILENCE

PRISM OF SILENCE

Editor

Pratyush Vatsala
Principal & Professor
Lakshmibai College
University of Delhi

&

Ratnakar Kumar
Assistant Professor
Lakshmibai College

KALPAZ

Published by

Kalpaz Publications
C-30, Satyawati Nagar,
Delhi – 110052
Ph.: 011-47034999, 9811692060
www.kalpazpublications.com
E-mail: kalpaz@hotmail.com

Distribution Network
gyanbooks.com
India, USA, Canada, UK, Australia, France

ISBN: 978-93-5722-405-5 (HB)
First Published, 2025

Printed at: Gyan Press, Delhi.

PRISM OF SILENCE
Editor: Pratyush Vatsala & Ratnakar Kumar

Contents

List of Contributors

Shayantani Das	Assistant Professor English, Hindu College, University of Delhi
Antara Bhatia	Assistant Professor English, Ramjas College, University of Delhi
Ratnakar Kumar	Assistant Professor English, Lakshmibai College, University of Delhi
Dr. Minakshi Kaushik	PhD English, JNU, Delhi
Kuntal Tamang	Associate Professor Department of English, Motilal Nehru College, University of Delhi
Sashi Teibor Laloo	Research Scholar, Department of History, North-Eastern Hill University, Shillong, Meghalaya
Ruqayya Bahar	Research Scholar, Department of English, Aligarh Muslim University
Somya	Assistant Professor, University of Delhi
Anjali Dawar	Ph.D. Scholar, Guru Gobind Singh Indraprastha University, Dwarka, University School of Humanities and Social Sciences
Dr. Chaandrayi Mukherjee	Assistant Professor English, Vivekanand College, University of Delhi
Dr. Prerana Sinha	Assistant Professor(Sr. Scale) Department of English, Atma Ram Sanatan Dharma College. University of Delhi, New Delhi

Introduction

I am Silence among secrets
Bhagavad Gita (Chapter 10:38)

Language function through the concept of 'sign', 'signifier' and 'signified' is well known. If a parallel is drawn between language and silence, then it is through the trope of voice of silence that a sound is heard of a syllable. 'Voiced' do exist on their own but when combined with 'voiceless' a meaningful utterance is created. The power of silence gets manifested in the utterances, we make. Without the pauses, meanings are chaotic. To decipher, to understand and to simplify, pauses are a must in a structure of a sentence. Concomitantly, if we expand our horizon, silence exists in our realm to give meaning to all voices around. The noise which we hear outside is meaningful only when clubbed with silence. On a macroscopic level, silence is the defining feature of all truths which we explore in this world. In other words, the truth is that inexpressible voice which we can never hear. It is the silence. Thus, 'Silence', 'Silencing', 'Silenced' are the defining features of human existence.

In the world of academics, the concept of silence has taken a prominence. The voices are no longer going to be silenced. The voices which were dominated and silenced for large amount of time have started to speak. The answer to the question of Spivak "Can the Subaltern speak?" is now in affirmation. A deconstructive approach to archives of literary work has gone to explore the tropes of silence. In the age of modernisation, it is apparent to locate such voices. Re-reading or re-visualising the past located in social-cultural-psychological sphere significantly exemplifies the absence as presence. An analysis into the works of Freud and Jung illuminates the world of silence through the realm of unconscious. Foucault's idea that non-existent entities are actually existing but in the power structure they are made to believe that they are non-existent is the base on which we can stablish the existence of the structure of silence.

Albeit, diligence must be taken that we don't create a cult of silence because as emphasised earlier, silence and voice function in relation to each other. In accordance with this understanding, this book **Prism of Silence**, records different voices manifested through silence. It is an ensemble of the essays on the theme of speaking silence. The scholars from different fields have contributed. The concept of silence is located through themes like – 'of violence in the realm of war and how silence functions through that', 'voices of silence coming through prison spaces', 'world of art capturing the moment of silence post-partition', 'the silenced voices of women writers in the performing space of Indian theatre' and many more.

In the first chapter, Shayantani Das looks at how prison writing emerges from the institutions of systematic silencing. The chapter focusses on the concept of 'I' regulated within the narratives. It attempts to give voices to silenced one. Antara Bhatia looks at the trope of silence and estrangement in the art of post-partition Pakistan. She explains that the sudden break from the cultural and social traditions of the past lead to isolation and a fragmented individual. The chapter explores that in detail.

Mr Ratnakar's chapter engages in understanding the silenced spaces in the age of modernism through the world of Detective literature and Modern texts. It exemplifies the relationship of silence in relation to war and gender. Minakshi Kaushik's work reflects on the women directors of Indian Theatre. It documents the silencing of women directors in the archives of Indian theatre located at various theatre and art institutions and looks at performance as a memory which is always alive.

Dr Shweta Saroha and Ms Himani Sharma reconnoitre the journey a woman take from the stage of adolescence to womanhood. It encapsulates the silenced voices resulting out of paedophilia. Ruqayya Bahar scrutinizes the patriarchy and its manipulation through close reading of *Blasphemy* by the Pakistani-British writer Tehmina Durrani and *My Name is Salma* by the Jordan based novelist Fadia Faqir.

If Kuntal Tamang's chapter probes historically the denial of voice to Kami, Damai and Saraki communities of Darjeeling and Sikkim, then Sashi's chapter examines the impact of partition on the lives of Khasi community of Meghalaya. Somya's text investigates the conception of silence, its politics and withholding the politics of violence by analysing MG Vassanji's *The Book of Secrets*. The awareness of colonialism, post-colonialism and neo-colonialism in the chapter is fragmented and there is a sense of hybridity.

The last three chapters of Anjali Dawar, Chandrayi Mukherjee and Prerna Sinha locates the concept of silence in Arundhati Roy's *The Ministry of Utmost Happiness*, Haruki Murakami's *Norwegian Wood*, Manto's short stories respectively.

The book through these chapters delves into the idea of speaking silence. The book highlights the voices which are hidden, unheard and silenced. However, only voices with no ears will mean nothing. It is important also to listen to these voices. This book is an attempt through which the voices will be listened. It is important to know that speaking silence is to be heard and listening others should be the final objective. Let us listen to the Silence around us to make this world more humane.

Editors

1

A Sisterhood of Silenced Voices: Analyzing Selected Prison Writing by Women in the Indian context

Shayantani Das

In the public consciousness, prisons exist as permanent and inevitable fixtures of our social landscape. Very rarely though do we look at these institutions as spaces of systematic silencing and rewriting of the prisoner's subject hood. In theory, these institutions are in place to administer punitive action while simultaneously being responsible for the rehabilitation of the "criminal". As Foucault talks about in *Discipline and Punish* (1975), the modern penal system marks a change from an earlier model of torture and public spectacle to a process that seeks to re-inscribe the criminal as "subject of law" (158). This new, seemingly benevolent model "no longer takes public responsibility for the violence that is bound up with its practice"(9). John Bender's work *Imagining Penitentiary* (1987) draws on Foucault and argues that in its conception of personality as malleable and capable of transformation, prison reform in England drew upon the emergent form of the novel and assumed "novelistic ideas of character" (69). He talks about how the stages of a prisoner's sentence resembled the different "stages of a classic plot" so that the prisoner would eventually arrive at a predetermined and desired stage of transformation (69). This metanarrative of the institution of prison seeks to first officially inscribe the subject as "criminal" through the processes of interrogation, trial and the language of law. The act of imprisonment itself is an act of silencing, subduing, and even curtailing potentially "subversive" activities. The justice system then also regulates and controls the prisoner's articulation of their own experience. Within the paradigm of the case-file, parole-system and the marks system wherein prisoners are rewarded for "good behaviour", the narrative of reform is the only one available to the prisoners effectively hijacking their own voices, disallowing them an official channel through which they can question the absoluteness of the state and its often-unfulfilled promises of non-arbitrariness and uniformity. In this paper, I look at how prison writing then emerges from within these institutions of systematic silencing. As a form of life-writing, this genre articulates an "I", a subject that is effectively writing from within a space that seeks to regulate their narrative. I specifically look at the category of political prisoners, which in its broadest definition would include those incarcerated "due to their active or passive involvement in political activities" (Wu 19) and their adoption of an authorial voice. By comparing Joya Mitra's *Hanyaman* published in 1989 during the Naxal uprising and Snehlata Reddy's *A Prison Diary* (1977)written during the emergency period, my work seeks to examine the articulation of the collective within the autobiographical, the use of language to express the inexpressible experiences of physical pain and torture and finally the protest against the grand narratives of criminality and reform that seeks to silence and confine to anonymity the voices of these women.

"I will die here slowly, like a forgotten song of the past" (10) writes Snehalata Reddy in *A Prison Diary,* which was published posthumously. It is a disjointed narrative published by the Human Rights Committee of the Karnataka State with heavy editorial intervention that put together specific excerpts from the journal she maintained and the letters she wrote when she was incarcerated without having committed a crime. As someone who was unjustly detained, incarcerated, denied proper healthcare, denied a recourse to justice even after her name was cleared and feared her imminent death, her voice is charged with the desire to act as a witness. Her narrative shows both her helplessness and the exercise of her agency. In spite of being a political prisoner arrested under the controversial MISA act, she was detained with Class C prisoners. Her diary abounds with her frustration with the institution where her knowledge of the law, her privilege as a well-known actress and an educated woman leads to nothing. She is repeatedly denied healthcare, she repeatedly writes that "I want an answer from the government" (12). She addresses official letters to superintendents, appeals to authorities and doctors but her efforts come to naught. But in spite of being thoroughly defeated mentally and physically, her narrative adopts an authorial voice when she acts as documentarian of the voices and names and stories of the women she is incarcerated with. In one instance she writes:

> "Noorjehan, 21 years old. Has a child four years old. Visited the cinema with her little daughter and her brother 12 years old. The police asked her to come to the police station. She refused saying why, they said we saw you soliciting. She said that was untrue. They took her to the van and asked her for Rs 150. She said she had only Rs 25. Then they said she could as well go to the court and booked her. Once they come here, they are branded as it were, and even if they go walking or to the cinema or anywhere they are nabbed." (15).

Her journal also records the specific ways in which the ill-treatment directed at her fellow prisoners is gendered in its nature. Describing their condition of forced labour, lack of recreation, exercise and proper nutrition she writes "Must women be treated worse than men even in the 20th century?"(16). Her work is a direct indictment of the reform model that the institution supposedly upholds. Reddy records that "As soon as a woman comes in, she is stripped naked in front of everyone else. When a human-being is sentenced, he or she is punished enough. Must the human body be degraded and humiliated as well? Who is responsible for these perverse methods?"(16). This critique of the official "power of writing", the language of the law and all its absurdities and meaninglessness is even stronger in Joya Mitra's work.

Unlike *A Prison Diary*, Joya Mitra's *Hanyaman* translated as *Killing Days: Prison Memoirs* by Shampa Banerjee is a memoir written after her release from jail. In it, the narrative voice moves back and forth between the present she inhabits and the past in the jail. In one moment, the "I" recollects memories of the past and says "the picture was still sharp in my mind, framed in twilight" (45), but within the space of a few paragraphs the "I" is a witness inhabiting the present tense - "I get into trouble with the jargon here" (46). The narrative blends the two to depict ways in which she is still living the past in her present and how the boundaries of prison move beyond physical dimensions. Her narrative too is charged with the responsibility of giving voice to the collective and to fight against the enforced anonymity of the institution. She acts as a witness and carefully represents the lived experiences of women which challenge and highlight the absurdity and violence of the language of prison rules. Her narratorial voice is charged with biting irony when she represents one such rule which is supposed to prevent self harm. Describing the state of a fellow inmate with mental illness she says – "But she wasn't given any clothes. No clothes are given to mad women. They may use it to hang themselves. And who'll be responsible for that? They came up with a novel solution- they covered half of the only door to the dark cell with a torn gunnysack" (107). This rule also allows a prison guard to brutally beat up another inmate who did not wish to be parted with a nail-cutter which was her treasured possession. Her narrative also highlights the various mechanisms of writing within the space of the prison. She recounts:

> "I watch the day's new prisoners coming into the hospital. The doctor checks their height, weight and identifying marks on a big card and signs it. That's what they call a 'ticket' here.

> Before that the prisoners are taken to the jailor to be entered into a log and be informed of their length of stay and reason of incarceration. This is called a 'case table'. Once I asked for a book, the Matron in charge of the woman's ward said "wait until you get a case table. And what kind of table is that". (23)

As a 21-year-old educated woman who got involved with the Naxal movement and is thus incarcerated, the narrative dwells on the peculiar position she occupies within the space of the prison. Her acts of protest include the writing of political slogans on the walls of the ward by rubbing leaves, till it is pointed out to her that most of her inmates can't read. The "I" in the present reconstructs her journey which started with the individual but moved towards the formation of a community and the articulation of collective voice that includes the subject positions of the variety of inmates she had- the unread and unlettered, the tribal, the sick, the old and the mad. But she doesn't occupy this authorial position with any kind of ease because of the nature of the experiences she is recollecting. She frequently declares that "I don't have a pen that can adequately describe the state inside..." (109). In *Regarding the Pain of Others* (2003), Sontag says "to photograph is to frame, and to frame is to exclude" (46), but Mitra deliberates frames her descriptions like photographs of atrocities which have the power to shock and disturb us, but also provides us with a direct expression of an event. She says:

> People who haven't witnessed the naked mad women of the female ward of Presidency Jail won't know most of the time that the two femur bones that come down the thighs from the wife pelvic bone in a woman's body have about eight inches of space between them. They won't know how completely denuded of flesh a starving body can be, and even after that what incredible ability it has to stay alive" (111)

Her narrative simultaneously records her experiences and highlights the impossibility of recording all that she witnessed. Or maybe it questions the readers ability to fully grasp her experience. As Elaine Scarry says in *Body in Pain* "Whatever pain achieves, it achieves in part through its unsharability, ... Physical pain does not simply resist language but actively destroys it." (6). Both narratives are marked by this dialectic- the impossibility of language when it comes to recording instances marked by such violence and pain directed at them or their fellow inmates and their bodies and the necessity for language to write an alternate record that challenges the official systematic silencing and revolts against the ideology of reform and punishment upheld by the institution of prison. It is also charged with the responsibility of being the voice of a collective that does not have access to language, literacy and writing, whose names, stories and pain will be forgotten and erased by official historiography.

In *Reading Autobiography* Sidonie Smith and Julia Watson define how a conversion narrative is one that "develops through a linear pattern—descent into darkness, struggle, moment of crisis, conversion to new beliefs and worldview, and consolidation of a new communal identity" (70). One can argue that the nexus of the case-file, parole and marks system that I spoke of in the beginning of my paper tries to enforce such a conversion narrative on the prisoners. From this perspective it is interesting to analyze ways in which Reddy and Mitra challenge or conform to this narrative. The thing that both narratives have in common is the lack of a linear journey or progression. Reddy's journals have dates but her writing talks about the suspension of time within the space of the prison. She writes:

> "30th August, 1976. Terrible days…
>
> In a real dark night of the soul, it's always there o'clock in the morning day after day. There were the times I wanted to die, really die." (11)

In Mitra's narrative, there is the formation of a communal identity that she reconstructs but her work subverts a linear pattern in even more ways than Reddy- whether it is through the construction of the 'I' that seamlessly moves between the past and present or her repeated disavowal of the experience of prison and its reform model as being meaningful in any way. In her work the self is constructed differently as it is a memoir. As political prisoners however, both narratives adopt what one can call an authorial voice, wherein remembering and bearing witness becomes a much-needed ethical act and an act of rebellion.

Mitra's narrative as a memoir speaks more about the failure of language and representation when it comes to representing the enormity and the inexplicability of her experience in jail and representing the voices of her fellow inmates. The driving force behind both narratives however is the necessity of memory, the necessity of recuperating the marginal voices which are always already under erasure, of being a responsible witness. Through the use of multivocality and experiments with fragmentations the self in the prison writing by Mitra is differently constituted. It is a self that writes and rewrites from within and against the narrative that tries to silence and erase their selfhood and that accepts the responsibility of the collective. In spite of being a work unintended of publication, Reddy's diary depicts similar questioning of the reform model and similarly performs the task of ethical witnessing through writing.

Works Cited

Bender, John. *Imagining the Penitentiary: Fiction and the Architecture of the Mind in Eighteenth Century England.* University of Chicago Press, 1989.

Foucault, Michel. *Discipline and Punish.* Penguin, 1979.

Mitra, Jaya. *Killing Days: Prison Memoirs.* Translated by Shampa Banerjee, Kali for Women, 2004.

Reddy, Snehalata. *A Prison Diary.* Bangalore: Human Right's Committee, 1977.

Scarry, Elaine. *The Body in Pain.* oxford University Press (N.Y. 1988).

Smith, Sidonie, and Julia Watson. *De/Colonizing the Subject: The Politics of Gender in Women's Autobiography.* Minneapolis: University of Minneapolis Press, 1992. Print.

Sontag, Susan. *Regarding the Pain of Others.* Farrar, Straus and Giroux, 2017.

Wu, Yenna, and Simona Livescu. *Human Rights, Suffering, and Aesthetics in Political Prison Literature.* Lexington Books, 2013.

2

Silence and Estrangement in post-partition Pakistani Art

Antara Bhatia

The art developments in twentieth century Muslim South Asia are full of turbulence and chaos. From 1947, with the Partition, multiple themes conflated in Pakistani art, from a revival of traditional forms to an introduction of modernist idiom. In other words, artists such as Zubeida Agha and Shakir Ali conflated contemporary modernist techniques, themes and motifs with their traditional Pakistani heritage, at the same time reworking the tradition and expressing their own individuality. The historical context of Pakistani visual arts following the decades of the 1920's- and 1930's is complex, schismatic and reflective of the changing social and political era, which is dominated by events such as the Partition of 1947, the liberation of Bangladesh in 1971, the rise of social media, the independence of Pakistan, decolonisation and an entry into a post-colonial world. More importantly, the formation of Pakistan as a nation-state was accompanied by much political turmoil, homelessness, pain and a sense of bafflement with the new world. There was an abrupt break, as it were, from the solid cultural traditions of the past, and it is at this historical juncture wherein takes place the complex interaction of modernity, modernism and South Asia. These events led to an increasing sense of isolation and fractured sense of self within individuals who had suffered the trauma of riots and dislocation.

Pakistan's political economy at the time was fractured, there was an ongoing financial crisis and any semblance of stability was left far behind with the death of the country's enigmatic leader, Mohammad Ali Jinnah. Any art emerging from this cultural chaos would truly be, as Jalaluddin Ahmed puts it, "crisis art" (*Art Today* 59). Crisis was constant, responses to it inevitable and imaginative. Post 1947 Pakistan lived through decades of almost constant disruption and change of regimes. Ayub Khan's decade, the declaration of Martial Law in 1958, followed later by the harsh political rule of General Zia-Ul-Haq and the subsequent civil unrest, parallel and intersect with the responses of Agha and other artists in their peculiar ways. In any case, the arts and humanities were in a defunct condition. In more concrete words, there was an attempt to wipe out intellectuals, artists, free-thinkers and others who were in 'danger' of introducing radical ideas into the impressionable public. This was carried out largely through the increasing persecution of the All Pakistan Progressive Writers Association, because it was full of activists and intellectuals conceived as a threat to the existing order. The crisis came to a head with the Rawalpindi Conspiracy Case (1951), which resulted in the Urdu poet Faiz Ahmed Faiz being jailed for four years. The deep, pervading sense of division and isolation in art arose in part from the abysmal condition of art schools and institutions and the departure of several artists from Lahore and Karachi to India. The centres of cultural activity, Lahore's Mayo School of Arts and the arts department in the Punjab University, faced the brunt of 1947 both in terms of students and faculty. Moreover, the humanities environment did not remain very conducive to radicalism, protest or modernism in the following years and frequent changes of the ruling order. Karachi, despite its positioning as a developing metropolis, did not have a specific platform for the arts till as late as 1953. Out of this chaos emerged the modernist group of artists Zainul Abedin (East Pakistan), Zubeida Agha and Shakir Ali. "New on the world stage, Pakistani artists aimed to present themselves as modern according to international standards. They adopted styles prevalent in Europe and the United States, but they also experimented with indigenous traditions to see how these could fit into the modern world" (Atteqa Ali, *Modern Art*). In the wider context of South Asian art, the various problems and crises of the modern world were at play. The rise of modernity had different phases in South Asia, particularly in India and Pakistan, both of which were directly suffering from the aftermath of the great divide. In the very momentous year of 1947, the Progressive Artists Group (PAG) was formed in Bombay. All the members of this group had radical leanings and rejected the traditional art of the Bengal School. This was a parallel to the re-appropriation of the Mughal school of art by the as well in the crossovers, there appear to be some parallel trends. One was the reworking of mythology, miniatures and what Hashmi calls "sentimental allegiances to the past" (13) exemplified by artists such as Ustad Allah Bux, A.R. Chughtai and Raja Ravi Verma, the last from India. Meanwhile, Shakir Ali, Agha and Rahamin Fyzee, along with the members of the Lahore Art Circle of the fifties including Hanif Ramay and Raheel Akbar Jamay, stayed clear of undue sentiment and instead used elements from the past to evolve a language of isolation, minimalism and modernismar ways.

The concept of *ajnabi* is a recurring one in Pakistani art, including that of Shakir Ali, Zubeida Agha, and later, Zahoorul Akhlaq and deeply connects their art. One of the leading proponents of activism and resistance through art, Zubeida Agha resonates through the post-Partition art scene. She evolved as an artist independently, regardless of the difficulties of art training for women in her milieu. She trained under the Italian prisoner-of-war Mario Perlingieri, who was in turn a pupil of Picasso's. Her art is a juxtaposition of the traditional and modern. Agha's paintings are distinctive in their depiction of interior landscapes. She uses colour and abstract forms to represent alienation. Her themes are echoed by other artists of the post-Partition period. There are conflicts not just with the world and the dizzyingly transforming society around them, but also with the self. Dadi remarks that both Shakir Ali's and Zubeida Agha's modernisms are constructed around "evasions and silences" (99). Both were immensely reticent and refused to discuss their creative viewpoint. Both discounted the realist style in favour of the modernist. They addressed questions about self and society, being a part of a profoundly divided, troubled milieu. They faced an abrupt disruption from the past and were propelled headlong into a new historical era. The most important similarity between them is that while both were dynamic art leaders, they were characterised by public silence and reticence. Hence, their art is full of silences; their refusal to speak translates into their art's refusal to 'speak' as it were. Thus, their paintings are entirely subject to the viewer's interpretation, a silence that is granted voice through a kind of viewer-response mechanism. Their subjects are fragmented, yet there is a relation between the various components, an internal sense of unity.

These artists are strangers in a milieu that represses art and is full of violence and schisms. In a sense, both are *ajnabi*; they withdraw into themselves and refuse to participate or voice their views. Their very silence renders them outsiders in their society. There is a deep sense of isolation in their paintings. Both deal with inner states of mind and a sense of relationship with the self. They reject any formulaic notions and instead focus on personal response to the angst and schisms of 20th century Pakistan. Both refuse to use verbal language to debate on issues of nationalism or the nation-state. Instead, they answer with application, practice and a non verbal language of their own. Referring to *Reclining Figure* (Fig. 1), the lone woman is emblematic of Agha's isolation as well as microcosmically, Pakistan's, the alienated and *ajnabi* positioning of both. The rootedness of the Mughal influence juxtaposes with the loneliness of the present here, symbolic of divides and silences.

Fig. 10. Zubeida Agha. *Reclining Figure.* n.d.

Metamorphosis (Fig. 2) is again an abstract mindscape, completely disjunct from reality and indicating change and a new order. Through the silence both in the works and in public, self-expression takes on entirely different overtones. It can be read politically as a form of protest, rather than as a retreat into interiority, simply because of the deliberate nature of the public refusal to elaborate on its assimilation into history using symbol and colour consciously seems to be a thrust towards subjectivity and multiple interpretation, a subtle response to crisis.

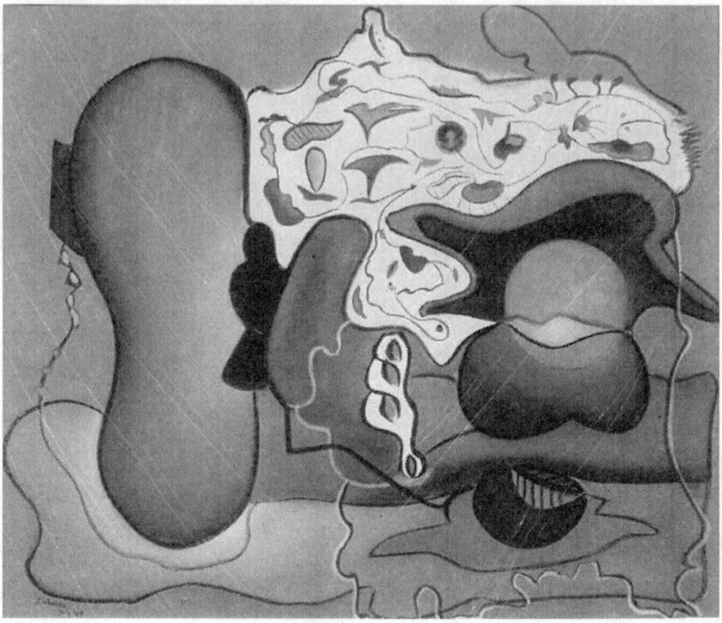

Fig. 2. Zubeida Agha. *Metamorphosis*. 1948.

Zubeida Agha and Shakir Ali, in Fig. 3 and Fig. 4 respectively, use modern artistic techniques to represent crisis. The abstraction of the paintings renders them open to multiple interpretations. Shakir Ali's painting is an amalgam of fragments. The gloom and jagged edges seem to be symbolic of the fractured nature of the milieu and society. Agha's fragments are full of vitality and brightly-coloured. However, lines and angles are used to show the brokenness of the subject. There are natural images, such as flowers, birds and leaves, but none of them are wholesome and are scattered all over the canvas, suggesting violence and divide. *Evening* ingeniously conflates isolation, fragmentation and loneliness in its depiction of Pakistan's urban cityscape and culture.

Ali's painting captures concrete industrial nature of the modern city in Pakistan and also the city in a state of fragmentation.

Fig. 3. Zubeida Agha. *Evening*. 1980.

Fig. 4. Shakir Ali. Untitled. n.d.

These artists thus use a highly individualised language to express the pain and anguish of their own selves and of their nation. Other artists have followed suit. In Lahore, and later Karachi, Ijaz-ul Hassan represented isolation in more overt modes of expression. His art can be seen as a silent protest against the repressive atmosphere of the Zia Ul Haq regime, through symbols of alienation. The feeling of estrangement is depicted by Hassan through his window series. The canvas evokes a feeling of being caged, looking out into a world that is dystopic, broken and gloomy (Fig. 5).

Fig. 5. Ijaz Ul Hassan. *View Through a Window.* 1980.

Zubeida Agha came to Karachi in 1953 and was fascinated with the cityscape. Many of her paintings thus appear to "reference skyscrapers or form what appear to be cityscapes- the inky dark structures with yellow squares of light seem to have been ingrained in her memory. They reflect the essence of the hustle and the bustle of such a city upon an individual- how one can feel overwhelmed and lonely all at once…" ("Zubeida Agha", *Khaas Gallery*). *Karachi by Night* (Fig. 6) is a composition that uses modernist laws of perspective. The bright lights of the city evoke a sense of gaiety and hustle-bustle; which is deceptive because the canvas is full of fragments and pieces. The painting evokes in synecdochic form the city of Karachi. It uses bright colours and yet uses modernistic techniques of fragmentation and linear perspective. There seems to be a deliberate attempt not to let the viewer's gaze comfortably rest at any point. The painting combines multiple perspectives, and contradictory ones. There is certainly a deep sense of nostalgia in the beauty of the city and the twinkling lights give it a lively evening feel. However, the fragmentation effect serves as a reminder that the city is fractured and morose after the Partition and the violence.

15. Karachi by night,
1956, oil on board (30" x 26.5")

Fig. 6. Zubeida Agha. *Karachi by Night.* 1956.

The silencing of women in the Islamic Republic since 1947 has been a much debated topic. Ayesha Jalal sees the positive and negative aspects of this paradigm.

> The relationship between women and the State in Pakistan has been both compelling and paradoxical. After nearly a decade of state-sponsored events at stifling women's voices in the public arenas and pushing back the boundaries of their social visibility, Pakistan became the first state in the Muslim world to have a woman Prime Minister.(Jalal qtd. in Hashmi 230).

This silencing became especially acute during the regime of General Zia-Ul-Haq. It can be traced back to the time of the great divide; the tragedy of which left indelible scars on both sides. Much of this suppression arose from the state of art education post 1947. The oldest centre was the Mayo School of Art, but which was entirely male, both in terms of faculty and students. It is Pakistani women artists that deploy this silence as resistant through art, poetry and

Fig. 7. Esther Rahim. *Danger.* 1961.

activism. In this politically charged and inhospitable environment, they subtly evolved a new language in art and painting. Influenced by global modernist methods of Cubism, abstractionism and linear perspective, their art remains deeply complex, difficult to unravel and yet expressive of the oppressive regime that seeks to silence them.

Hashmi remarks that "A major aspect of Zia's rule was its special targeting of minorities and women. The erosion of women's status in law and public life found a response in their activism and their art" (*Memory, Metaphor, Mutation* 23). Esther Rahim's *Danger* (Fig. 7), painted in 1961, the same year that Agha moved to Rawalpindi, allegorises the horror and fear of the totalitarian governments and political crossroads.

Agha, on the other hand, responded through abstractionism and estrangement. *Carnival* by Agha (Fig. 8) again uses space according to the laws of physics, suggesting order within the chaos. According to Dadi, *Carnival* is composed of "bright and twisted organic shapes, precise, flat and complex and set against a flattened geometric plane, suggestive of a scientific schema of cells or some other complex organism whose elements are in dynamic tension, depicted in an abstract space" (116).

Agha uses scientific principles and physical space to express her own notion of reality. Here again the Cubist style of fragmentation is evident, and the subject is broken up into tiny pieces, possibly an influence of Picasso but re-appropriated through an individual metaphor and her signature use of colour profusions. It provides multiple perspectives on the same subject, to show the immense complexity of the modern post war world. She practices discipline and distancing in her art and does not get caught in an emotional vortex. For Agha, there is the use of estrangement or an alienation effect but also, as Dadi remarks, "harmony and reconciliation within the picture plane" (117). None of her canvases, thus, are entirely anarchic or chaotic. This may well have reflected a positive hope for harmony in her fractured, suffering milieu.

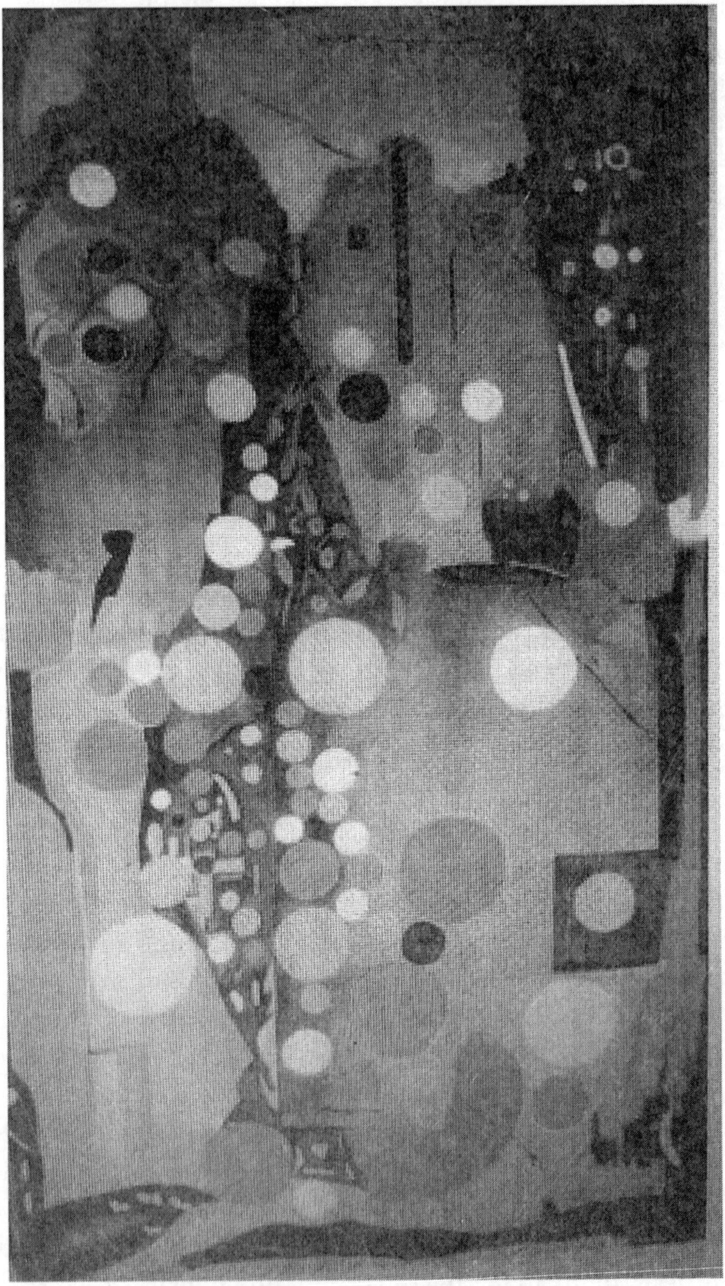

Fig. 8. Zubeida Agha. *Carnival.* 1978.

Pakistanti artists thus symbolically represented the concept of ajnabi, which also can be interpreted as the state of Pakistan vis-à-vis its relationship with the world post 1947. The language of individuality and subtle resistance continues till today, irrespective of repressive regimes and multiple attempts to silence the artistic voice.

Works Cited

Ahmed, Jalaluddin. "Art Today in Pakistan." *Modern Art of Asia: New Movements and Old Traditions*. Ed. Japan Cultural Forum. Japan: Toto Shuppan Company, 1961. 59-64.

Ali, Atteqa. "Modern Art in West and East Pakistan." *Heilbrunn Timeline of Art History*. New York: Metropolitan Museum of Modern Art, 2000. Web. 1. 7. 2017.

Dadi, Ifthikar. *Modernism and the Art of Muslim South Asia*. USA: North Carolina University Press, 2010.

Dalmia, Yashodhara and Salima Hashmi. *Memory, Metaphor, Mutations: Contemporary Art of India and Pakistan*. New Delhi: Oxford University Press, 2007.

Hashmi, Salima. "An Intelligent Rebellion: Woman Artists of Pakistan". *India International Centre Quarterly*. Vol. 24, No. 2/3. www.jstor.org/stable/23005448.

"Zubeida Agha." 2016. *Khaas Gallery.* Web. 1. 7. 2017. <http://khaasgallery.com/artist/zubeida-agha/>.

Paintings

—. *Evening*. 1980. Web. 12. 7. 2017. <https://www.dawn.com/news/1158908>.

__.*Karachi by Night.* 1956. Web. 12.7.2017.<https://thesaproject.wordpress.com/2013/05/14/the-darker-the-night-the-shinier-the-lights/>

__.*Metamorphosis*. 1948. Web. 4.10.2017. <http://khaasgallery.com/artist/zubeida-agha/>.

__. *Reclining Figure*. n.d. Memory, Metaphor, Mutations: Contemporary Art of India and Pakistan. By Dalmia and Hashmi. New Delhi: Oxford UP, 2007. p. 16. Print.

Ali, Shakir. *Untitled.* n.d. Web. 12. 7. 2017. <Vasl Artists' Collective>.

Hassan, Ijaz-Ul. *View Through a Window*. 1980. Web. 04.10.2017. <https://www.ijazulhassan.com>.

Rahim, Esther. *Danger*. 1961. Memory, Metaphor, Mutations: Contemporary Art of India and Pakistan. By Dalmia and Hashmi. New Delhi: Oxford University Press, 2007. p. 42. Print.

3

Politics of Silence in relation to War in Detective Fiction: Understanding the interrelationship between War and Gender through Agatha Christie's *The Mysterious Affair at Styles* & *N or M?* and Virginia Woolf's *Three Guineas*

Ratnakar Kumar

The modern age is remembered for the Two Wars: the two wars in the literal sense as well as the war within the different spheres of the world. These social, economic, cultural spheres of the world was very much affected by the happenings in another world- a world in which nations were fighting for the pride and the honour. This paper is not going to address these issues, neither it is going to do a study of these wars and see how the social structure is affected because of war, leading to the disturbances within the society, but it is going to study a space which is created, not in the response to the war, as modernist sensibilities are, instead a space which is trying to escape or somehow ignore the fact that there is any war going outside the realm of its space or a space which is in fear of war and so tries to give minimum space to it; a space which is silent on war. This space which decided to remain silent towards the war, is a space created by detective novels. This space I will like to call a feminine space (a space which speaks only in silence) and in contrast to this space is war battlefield which I will term as masculine space. Masculine space of war can be defined as a space where things are not investigated; no punishment for the murder, even when we know the murder is not of one individual but the mass murder where as the feminine space of detective fiction can be a space where if a murder takes place, there is a complete silence. There is no celebration as we see on the other side - war. It becomes essential according to the norms of social structure that the peace is restored, and usually by a male detective. In the world of patriarchy, everything done by a male is overlooked and there is no punishment where as in the same world, a woman is silenced and she is always under scrutiny and suspicion. This politics of silence needs to be read in the context of war and gender. Silencing the other has been the defining feature of war, and gender roles have also been designated in the same context. In this context, if we imagine the world irrespective of any boundary, we will notice that this world is a patriarchal world; patriarchy functioning not only within the domestic space but also outside it in a metaphorical way. Even the world of literature functions as a patriarchal one. Detective genre, considered to be un-worthy by the modernist, was read by women readers.

The question of whether calling a space feminine is an attempt to reassert the masculinity in that space or an attempt to define its own space in order to subvert that masculine reassertion is debatable. I think both the arguments hold true to certain context. There is no doubt that masculinity is reasserted by the detective figure by placing things in order but at the same time, if I go back to the argument about the treatment of a detective space as a space which has the attitude of indifference toward the war and has opted to remain silent on it, I would like to bring Virginia Woolf's idea in *Three Guineas* of showing "indifference" to war "by the daughters of educated men… to prevent war". Cacophony around the war produces more war; silence silences the war. It will be problematic to say that Agatha Christie's works are in alignment with the idea expressed by Woolf but the attitude of indifference towards the war is very much explicit in her first novel, *The Mysterious Affair at Styles*. The novel which goes on to mention war at two to three instances in the start completely overlooks the war as novel progresses and dedicates solely towards the crime and concern of the characters as well as the reader in knowing the criminal. The very start of the novel affirms this attitude by showing how this world is going to forget the war sooner. Captain Hastings describes "as one looked out over the flat Essex country, lying so green and peaceful under the afternoon sun, it seemed almost impossible to believe that, not so very far away, a great war was running its appointed course. I felt I had suddenly strayed into another world" (13). This is the feeling a reader gets towards the end of the novel that he had inhabited another world- a world which is not only different from the real world but also a world which is different from the previous worlds visited by the reader; a world which is created by a female author; a world which is always trying to answer the issue of gender biasness in this crime world; a world whose silence on war is concomitant with the gender which is silenced in the world. The aspect of silence in relation to war in detective fiction and its relation with gender will be studied in this paper by looking at two texts of Agatha Christie, *The Mysterious Affair at Styles* &*N or M?* and her contemporary Virginia Woolf's *Three Guineas.*

The critics have gone to debate about the world of Christie and most of them sees a nostalgia toward pre-war world and sees Christie as someone holding on to the conventional framework of domestic space. Merja Makinen, in the book *Agatha Christie: Investigating Femininty*, says in the context of "Christie's critical reception in the context of gender", "The focus for Christie has been more on her as a 'conservative' writer reinforcing stereotypes rather than contesting them" (09). Makinen, herself, is not of this opinion and sees a different and subversive treatment of femininity in case of female villains. I agree with her point of view that Christie draws the equality between a male and female villain. Christie subverts the notion of a female murderer as fore-grounded by earlier writers. For example, we notice in Baroness Orczy's "The York Mystery" that a woman can commit a crime only on the basis of love as "women when they love, think only of one object on earth – the one who is beloved". Christie very cunningly subverts this. The woman who commits murder is the least suspected because of the garb of being a conventional female figure. She is no longer conventional but just pretends to be that. Woman uses that power of being conventional. Using the domesticity provided by the patriarchy to hide the real motive. It is more of a performance. It is "reiteration of a set of norm or set of norms, to the extent that it acquires an act-like status in the present, it conceals or dissimulates the convention of which it is a repetition" (Butler 12). It is not that Christie completely revolutionize the figure of woman but she gives her woman a modern sensibility. It will be unfair to pin down the subversion only in the case of villains but it is also seen in the portrayal of other women characters. In *The Mysterious Affair at Styles*, it is revealed by the end by Mrs Cavendish that she has been forced into this world of Cavendish by the death of her father. Otherwise, she would not have preferred this idle life of being the wife of a noble man. She says, "When I was twenty-three, I had been nearly all over the world. It was a splendid life – I loved it". The sense of freedom which one notices here is very much similar to the sense of freedom expressed by Virginia Woolf for those women who can earn the guinea. Woolf says that the woman "no longer use her charm to procure money from her father or brother". A woman in this modern world has "the deep breath of freedom". Women began to desire for a free existence and not always desiring to marry; even going to the extent of leaving the husband. When Captain Hasting ask Mrs Cavendish whether she is going to leave John, she answers, "Perhaps – because I want to be free!" (223).

The problem with Christie, I think, is that after giving the agency, she takes it back from her female characters. In her first novel, just for the sake of uniting the couple, she makes his detective allow the trial of an honest person in order to restore the "conjugal happiness" and make his male detective say, "The happiness of one man and woman is the greatest thing in all the world" (296). Further, there are certain instances in the text where the crime and murder are defined according to gender convention. Mrs Cavendish says that murder can be associated with women in the "case of poisoning" (19). So, when murder takes place, we know one thing for sure that murderer has to be a female as the murder is supposed to have taken place with the help of poison. The feature of domestic space is used by the villains to commit the murder and that space also goes on to draw the distinction between a male murderer and the female one. Mrs Cavendish above statement comes in reaction to the statement made by Miss Howard that "murder's a violent crime. Associate it more with a man" (19). If one takes this into account then one will notice that the statement of Mrs Cavendish function both as reaffirmation of gender biasness by categorising the process of committing the murder and as denial of strictness of masculinity of being violent. This denial of 'masculinity of being violent' is reflective of the increase in the tolerance of violence in domestic space, may be because of outside war; this tolerance is also among the readers and so we notice tolerance towards violent ending as in *N or M?*. In spite of the fact that detective novels choose to remain silent on war and its violence and show tolerance with respect to that, war has gone to manifest itself through silence.

Furthermore, female violence is not so much in showing physical prowess but in scheming the things in such a way that the detection will come as surprise, not only for the reader but also for the detective. Thus, in this feminine space of detective fiction, any disorder appears as surprise and so the disturbance where as in war space, the element of surprise is lost and thus a monotonous life. Detective novels, because of being best sellers, have to remain silent on war because the element of monotony cannot be acceptable in this genre and it thrusts upon the element of surprise. Ironically, this world of detective fiction is freer in comparison to the canonical ones. They have the freedom to remain silent on war and thus making the war, an irrelevant phenomenon. However, the modernists were doomed to talk about war to show how great the modernists are. In Styles, the similar kind of life is inhabited by Mrs Cavendish. She is constantly in war with John Cavendish and thus wishing to break free. John Cavendish being a male, representative figure for any war, never realises that need for freedom and is satisfied with the monotonous life. It appears as if detective fiction is in war with war by refusing to give any space to it in its narrative and in contrast to this, modernists are in love with the war. Ironically, the great modernists will not be great ones if there was no war. However, detective fiction will thrive on its own, in the presence or the absence of war. In the same way, woman is free because she is not functioning in reference to a context. The man is bound to function with respect to the context.

The question arises whether that freedom is possible to attain in the historical framework of gender in that age. War, somehow helped to break the boundaries but at the same time emphasis had increased on the domesticity of the woman. Women began to have the illusionary power in the house in the absence of conventional male figure but in reality they had no power. With the ending of the war, the power of a woman within the house and also those women who were working as nurse in the battlefield will be lost as there will be no wounded body to be taken care of. Is this true or in the words of Butler, "its theatricality gains a certain inevitability given the impossibility of a full disclosure of its historicity" (12-13)?

Furthermore, during the war, the soldiers who got wounded returned back to the domestic world. It will be interesting to point out that these persons, in the absence of the masculine space, try to create that space within the domestic world. This creation will lead to a further creation of a new space which will be conglomeration of the two spaces which we have talked about. This new creation within the domestic world is the creation resulting from the failure of the masculinity in the war field. This failure allows the movement from the war space to this domestic space. With the ending of World War I, war had taken shape within the domestic space and had started influencing the domestic sphere. Even, in the case of detective novel, it began to help in solving the puzzle. For example, in *The Mysterious Affair at Styles*, Poirot's conclusion about the Will, not been destroyed, is based on the practice of "War economies... at Styles"; according to which "no waste paper was thrown away. There was, therefore, no means of destroying a thick document such as a will" (268).

As war had already entered the domestic space, World War II was no longer an exclusive masculine space. It was no longer an outside happening to be neglected. The Great War had already taken place and disturbed the inner space of the world. So, with the coming of World War II, the outside and inside started to merge. War was no longer an issue to be dealt outside but started to creep into inner space in the form of spies and most dangerously by making friends from within. In the context of being a patriot, these spy figures were not doing anything wrong but now with the issue of nation, the equation of crime and its detection changed. The fatal threat was from within. Since, the threat was from within, the inner space occupant had to take the responsibility of the proceedings and solve the case. This is very much evident in the characterisation of Tuppence in Christie's novel *N or M?* The coming of a female detective is no doubt a threat to the masculine authority of the feminine space. The threat is very much evident in Mr. Grunt's attitude towards Tuppence. He only wishes Tommy to go for investigation. Just imagine, if Tuppence is absent in the process of detection, what would have been the consequences. In fact, she becomes the great detective in the end instead of Tommy as she is someone to get the hold of M by the logical deduction whereas Tommy is able to find N by luck.

The detective here is not alone but in is in pair. The pairing is very much different from previous coupling of male and female detective. Here the work is done together and this notion of togetherness is asserted lot of times. So, the merging is of both the spaces. Masculinity and femininity merge together to create a new space, androgynous space, in order to deal with the problem. This new space is also created in the relationship of detective figures. The pairing of Tommy and Tuppence is a kind of androgynous pairing where the suffering, earlier which was majorly associated with one among the pair like Watson and Hasting, is now somehow shared. This sharing is no doubt not a uniform one and is more of a necessity. The merging is necessary because the enemy from within can be located only by that person who is part of that space. In this context, Virginia Woolf's *Three Guineas* unanswered question to a female by a male becomes important. The question, "How in your opinion are we to prevent war?" is a valid question to a female if we agree with this coming together of the two spaces- masculine and feminine, making masculinity of femininity and femininity of masculinity.

My paper does not allow me to dwell more in the novel *N or M?* and point out the issues in relation to gender and gender stereotyping still present in this new world but these cannot be neglected at any point in the text. Besides, masculinity of femininity is an exceptional quality to be found (it can be termed exceptional because the masculine world is exposed to only those females who were somehow serving the soldiers in the war) whereas femininity of masculinity is a characteristic of male detective in Golden - Age crime fiction. Heather Worthington in the book *Key Concepts in Crime Fiction* says, "The 'feminisation' of the male detective is a strong element in Golden-Age crime fiction … This is perhaps in response to the growing number of female writers and readers of crime fiction in this period, and can be related back to World War I and the hundreds of thousands of men killed in action, leaving a population in Britain in which women heavily outnumbered men" (47).

In conclusion, I would like to highlight that merging of space did happen in the world of literature. Detective novels are now studied in the canonical context and canonical are investigated with the lens of a detective. You need to read against the grain. This deconstructive approach allows us to read the politics of silence in detective fiction and at the same time, it throws light on (in ironic sense) love for war in modernist texts. The quintessence of the argument is that silence speaks for itself, but when it does, we are supposed to remain silent. Cacophony of sound is not supposed to silence the music of silence.

Works Cited

Butler, Judith. *Bodies That Matter*. New York & London: Rouledge, 1993. Print.

Christie, Agatha. *N or M?* New Delhi: Thomson Press India Ltd., 2001. Print.

—. *The Mysterious Affair at Styles*. Noida: Gopsons Papers Ltd., 2007. Print.

Makinen, Merja. *Agatha Christie: Investigating Femininity*. New York: Palgrave Macmillan, 2006. Print.

Orczy, Baroness. *The Old Man in the Corner*. Steven desJardins and PG Distributed Proofreaders. The Project Gutenberg, 1 January 2004. EBook.

Woolf, Virginia. *Three Guineas (1938)*. 1. Don Lainson dlainson@sympatico.ca. A Project Gutenberg of Australia, November 2002. EBook.

Worthington, Heather. *Key Concepts in Crime Fiction*. New York & London: Palgrave Macmillan, 2011. Print.

4

The Silence of The Archive, Performance as a Living Memory: A Case of Women Directors in Indian Theatre

Minakshi Kaushik

In the research on historiography of women directors in Indian theatre, there emerges a very self-reflexive criticality in the methodology in that though the work would have liked to be more comprehensive and inclusive or attempt to retrieve more lost and marginalised work of women directors, the problem of archives and sources persisted. Diana Taylor's theorisation around the documented "archive" and the oral "repertoire" (*The Archive and the Repertoire*, 2003) is testimony to the erasures that historical records of performance traditions quite often inevitably produce. In such a scenario, this paper seeks to trace the nature and the ideological underpinnings of the silence that operates in the documentation of women directors' practices and productions in Indian theatre in the archives of The National School of Drama, Sangeet Natak Akademi, Natya Shodh Sansthan, Natrang Pratishthan and National Centre for Performing Arts.

The methodology will be trace how vis-à-vis this absence or insufficiency, oral memory or repertoires of their works; or their personal collections serve as an unofficial redressal or rather exposure of State mediated histories of Indian theatre. Against the marginalisation in archives, repeated performances of works directed by these women in the past, for instance, serve as an affective mode of audience relationality that, through repetition, establishes a living memory versus the selective history that creates a canonical tradition of the narrative of a Nation.

In much the same manner, the em-bodi-ment of these practices is a gendered subversion by these women directors since what is conventionally seen as the site of marking out, or marginalisation of a woman's identity, that is, the body, here becomes a medium of performative repetition and reiteration of practices and a liveness that disappear even as they appeared. In so doing, these women directors emphasise the transitoriness or artifice of archives and how the silence regarding women directors is an enforced one. Yet they demonstrate how it is in disappearing and reappearing, that silences are manifested, even though they may not be reconstructed. As Odai Johnson puts it in 'The Size of All That's Missing', "the heart of the historiographical problem is ... how to ... allow the missing a chance to be present again." (3).

The National School of Drama houses only such work as has been part of its festivals, student or Repertory productions. The festivals often showcase its own plays or even for those from outside, they end up creating a certain image of what theatre is or what 'Indian theatre' is. Such documentation excludes the other alternative kinds of theatre happening around by various groups or individuals. Also, it disregards theatre happening at the regional level that takes up regional concerns. The alternative theatres are often subversive of State and especially the Centre's policies. In particular, in terms of women's productions, mostly such work is available that has been directed by women directors working for the institution. Such a practice is elitist and the various aspects of gender concerns manifesting in different regions are evaded.

In addition, the work that even these women have done outside the fold of the institution is not recorded here. Such archiving, therefore gives only a partial insight into the multiplicity of theatre forms happening in the country and also creates a singular narrative of a particular kind of work. This archiving hence leads to a silencing of other dimensions of theatre.

In terms of historical periodisation, there is more coverage in the archives of the Sangeet Natak Akademi in that there are older works also present which is not the case in NSD. Some of the Assamese woman director Rabijita Gogoi's plays and Sheila Bhatia's works for instance in this collection. However, it is not as inclusive as it could or should have been and here too, one finds the reproduction of canons such the Nehru Shatabdi NatyaSamaroh. Jill Dolan, in *The Feminist Spectator as Critic* (1988) argues in favour of a materialist-feminist, apparatus-based study which reads the ideological bias of theatre and denaturalises gender. She also discusses how a canon is "reified", in which context, women's works are solely judged on the basis of universality. In other words, canons tend to be self-perpetuating. Once a trend of documentation is established, similar works tend to be privileged and it leads to a cyclical process where the archival canon just reproduces itself and offers a monolithic view of theatre practices. Both NSD and SNA documentation of male directors' works such as B. V. Karanth's or Chandrashekhar Kambar's suggest a male centric view of Indian theatre history as this archiving becomes the basis of writing theatre histories.

The personal collections of Nemichandra Jain and Rekha Jain converted into the Natrang Pratishthan located in Ghaziabad. Although women directors such as Anuradha Kapur, Neelam Mansingh Chowdhry, Anamika Haksar and Vijaya Mehta get covered here, many other significant figures are left out. For somebody like Mehta, again, quite a few of the interviews etc are through events organized by the Pratishthan itself. While newer or those figures outside the folds of metropolis' are excluded, the archiving becomes a coterie of select figures, silencing the already marginalised voices.

Regional-base archives cater to regional interests and cover geographical area-specific work which may or may not be available in the archives of the capital or NCR. In that sense, they add significantly to redress the bias of the latter. The NatyaShodhSansthan, for instance, stores the works of several women directors of Kolkata, both contemporary as well as those from older generations. However, in such collections too, at times, for instance in the National Centre for Performing Arts in Mumbai, very few works and that too by a major canonical figure of a woman director such as Vijaya Mehta are recorded, making a vast body of her as well as other women's works, inaccessible.

In contrast, most of the women directors maintain their own personal collections of plays directed by them, as one has witnessed in the case of Usha Ganguli's collection at her studio Rangakarmee, Anamika Haksar's, Maya Rao's, Neelam Mansingh's and for many more at their own houses. Such records are privately circulated amongst friends and scholars. They retain a status of personal value and the exchange exceeds the officialdom of other archives which circulate in the public space. The traversing from public to private spaces and often to the public again, blurs the neat dichotomisation of women's labour. The archiving itself showcases the process of forced relegation of women's labour to the private domain which here, however, is a deliberate act that does not subsume the labour into anonymity. It instead begins a whole new process of circulation of these works for study or inspiration for further productions and the process of creation and circulation negotiated with viewing by all kinds of audiences in the public again in the outside public domain undergirds and exposes the very process by which these women practitioners' labour is quite often denied public recognition in official records.

Apart from this, several older plays by these directors get performed repeatedly again and again. It is both a revival for current pertinence as well as the creation of a personal memory against an official history. Usha Ganguli staged *Badnam Manto* again in 2016, and *Hum Mukhtara* several times in the past few years,

Kirti Jain revived *Suvarnalata* in 2019, Maya Rao has been consistently re-performing *Walk*, to name a few. To take up *Walk* as an instance, it has appeared as a protest/activist performance against the Nirbhaya rape case of 2012, it has differently manifested as a solidarity performance against Article 377 or one on Parliament Street on Valentine's Day to subvert the misogynistic image-construction that happens during such an event. These performances which survive as live memory are therefore a resistance against being documented in archives that exclude the gender ideology encased in these productions. Their oral circulation as repertoire is a refusal to be categorised as official record and instead builds its own narrative of the discontent that gender-based exploitation instigates. The false narrativisation of Nation building initiated by male-dominated practices and directions is thereby undercut, exposing the insufficiency of State rhetoric.

In a personal interview conducted in May 2019, Anuradha Kapur mentions that one of the cornerstones for her theatre work has been to bring women as performers to the public space. If Joseph Roach's "surrogation" (*Cities of the Dead*, 1996) is for past practices or rituals to exist in present performances, women directors' orally circulating repertoires are a "surrogation" meant to re-inscribe the disappearing bodies of women as performers in public spaces (through theatre) for them to be able, as actors, to embody the performance as a live experience that exists only within the rubric of the performance. The performing body is in excess, an excess that resists archiving, an excess that conveys the silence of the archive in its orality.

Works Cited

Dolan, Jill. *The Feminist Spectator as Critic*. Ann Arbor: UMI Research Press, 1988.

Johnson, Odai. 'The Size of All That's Missing'. University of Michigan Press, 2018. 1-43.

Roach, Joseph. *Cities of the Dead*. Columbia University Press, 1996.

Taylor, Diana. *The Archive and the Repertoire*. Durham: Duke University Press, 2003.

5

Denying the Dalit Identity: the Silence of the Kami, Damai, and Saraki Communities of Darjeeling and Sikkim

Kuntal Tamang

The Nepali speaking community is spread across Nepal, Bhutan, western Himalayan states of India, and eastern India. In India, the community is particularly concentrated in Sikkim and adjoining Darjeeling where it forms an overwhelming majority. The community, also known as Gorkha, comprises of many sub-castes and sub-groups with a mixed composition of those who are part of the varna system on the one hand, and non-varna tribal and other sub-groups on the other. Those within the varna system are stratified as per the Manu code.

For the purpose of this paper, I will limit myself to an examination of the Dalit narrative, or the lack of it, within the Indian Nepali speaking community of India, particularly that of Darjeeling district and Sikkim. A primary reason for this limited scope is the different historical trajectories the community has had in Nepal and in India. The Indian Nepali speaking community has been part of the British India and Independent India while the Nepalese counterpart of the community has been part of a monarchical dispensation until very recently. Also, despite shared linguistic and cultural heritage, the Indian counterpart has focussed on developing and strengthening its Indian identity as distinct from that of the Nepalese.

According to the 2011 Census of India, Sikkim has a little less than 5% Scheduled Castes while Darjeeling has about 17%. In both of these areas, and more so in Darjeeling, the community, although comprising of many caste and non-caste groups, has asserted a unitary 'Gorkha' identity that denotes all of the sub-groups in one category. This assertion has gained increasing strength from the Gorkhaland movement that began in the 1980s and has revived and continued with intensity since 2007. One of the questions this paper will examine is the ways in which the strong and overarching Gorkha discourse affected the Dalit discourse among the Nepali speaking people of these areas.

On 3rd March 2019 a meeting of the Kami, Damai, and Sarki communities (the three Scheduled Castes of the Indian Nepali speaking people) was held in Siliguri. Delegates of these communities from Nepal and India participated in the meeting. The delegates resolved to form an International Forum with a thirty-member drafting committee that was entrusted with the responsibility of framing the structure and scope of the organisation. What is significant, however, is that the Forum, after deliberations and insistence from the Indian delegates, decided not to use the term "dalit" to identify themselves. The Indian delegates believed that they could not relate with "Dalit", which, they thought, signified the image of a "poor person in dire straits that we get to see from the rest of India" (Sharma).

Binay Gazmer, one of the drafting committee members of the Forum, insisted that the lot of the Kami, Damai, Sarki (KDS) community was much better than that of Dalits. "It (dalit) gives the picture of a very miserable state of living which is not exactly the status of the KDS among the Nepali speaking people. We feel most comfortable using the term *'Anusuchit Jati'* (Scheduled Caste) as provided in the Indian Constitution." Gazmer, who is also the president of the Isai (Christian) KDS, however, does not deny discrimination against the KDS community both within the Nepali speaking community at large and the Christian Nepali community. This discrimination, according to him, may not be apparent in routine interactions or within church meetings but is certainly manifested in matrimonial considerations and in important social gatherings.

Shekhar Sewa, the convenor of the International Forum and the president of the All Sikkim Scheduled Caste Welfare Association, is also very certain about not using the term "Dalit" for the KDS community. According to him, the term is not recognised in Sikkim and Scheduled Caste is a more acceptable and "respectable" term. Both Sewa and Gazmer are aware of the powerful assertion of Dalit identity in India and Nepal but insist that the lot of the Indian KDS is not reflected in the "pessimistic" term Dalit. Another argument forwarded by Gazmer was that the International Forum would connect with the global KDS community which might include members from countries that have no history or context of caste based discrimination. Such members would not be able to relate to the Dalit experience. With global network as the primary aim of the Forum, the committee members felt that focus on culture and heritage would be the appropriate approach for building a global collective.

While the purpose of these two leaders is essentially discovering cultural heritage and instilling pride in it, there are others such as Mithilesh Baraily, a young urban Kami activist from Kalimpong (until recently part of Darjeeling), who assert their caste identities by suffixing their caste as a title to their names. Kamis are blacksmiths whose most iconic creation is the *Khukuri*- the curved machete that is the globally recognised symbol of Gorkha valour and pride. Despite creating the most powerful cultural symbol of the Nepali speaking Gorkhas, the Kamis find no pride of place within the community. Baraily added the title "Kami" to his social media profile as an act of assertion of his caste identity. By introducing himself as a Kami, Baraily draws sharp focus to his daily lived experience as a stigmatised member of the community. His unabashedly presented Kami identity is a cause of discomfort to the people he meets in social gatherings and inter-personal interactions as the word Kami, like Damai and Sarki, is considered unutterable in polite circles. Kamis have other less "offensive" sounding and "respectable" titles to introduce their caste when asked. But Baraily's introduction of himself as a Kami disrupts the social strategy that denies discriminatory caste stratification. Narrating his experience on being asked about his caste in weddings, where caste identities are strongly played out, Baraily says, "I calmly say 'Kami' and not Biswakarma (the polite form that people increasingly use these days) and suddenly the mood of the place changes and people give awkward looks. Sometimes they even say, 'Oh sorry! Sorry bhai...didn't mean to hurt.' As if I'm suffering from some kind of affliction" (Sharma). Baraily's personal campaign has found support among other members of the community who sent him messages of support. Some of them followed him and added 'Kami' to their social profile names as an attempt to exorcise the burden of guilt and shame that the members of the community have about themselves.

Binayak Sundas, a young academic with university degrees from St. Stephen's College and JNU, also embarked on the project of overcoming caste shame and stigma. He wrote an article titled "I am a Damai and I am Proud of it" in a popular social media page called *The Darjeeling Chronicle*. Damais are traditionally tailors and musicians of the Nepali speaking community. The *Naumati Baja*, a group of nine traditional music instruments played together, is played by the Damais at the head of marriage processions and other important events and is considered auspicious. Nevertheless, Damais are subjected to all the discrimination that dalits face everywhere else. Sundas says that when he typed the word "Damai" for the article, he felt "mildly ashamed". It is in engaging with his own identity that he learnt that he had been conditioned to be ashamed of himself and that he could break the shackles of the caste system only by breaking free of the stigma that he had internalised.

For members of the community, assertion of dignity involves highlighting the rich heritage and culture of the KDS community. Since the *Khukuri* and the *Naumati Baja* are high heritage symbols of the Nepali speaking people, the KDS community asserts pride by laying claim to these very symbols. Sewa, the president of All Sikkim Scheduled Caste Association, is also the founder of an organisation that has revived the *Naumati Baja* tradition amongst the youth and is working towards preserving this heritage in order to inculcate *Jatiya* pride in the richness of the culture.

This complex negotiation of KDS identity involving assertion of caste heritage and pride on the one hand and unwillingness to be identified with Dalits on the other is an expression of the internalisation of the dominant discourse that denies discrimination. The invisiblisation of caste discrimination is a strategy of the upper castes to ensure there is no mobilisation against caste hierarchy. The KDS assertion that their lot is not bad enough for them to be called Dalits is what Gopal Guru refers to as the effect of 'relative deprivation' in his essay 'The Dalit Movement in Mainstream Sociology' (135).This relative deprivation isolates "the Dalits under reference from the large Dalitness....tends to prevent the formation of a critical consciousness" (140). The 'relative deprivation' combined with the narrative of greater 'Gorkha Unity' has ensured that no concrete Dalit discourse has effectively developed among the KDS. Any sub-group or caste identity based assertion is seen as a challenge to this unity.

The resistance to the emergence of any discursive space other than the overarching Gorkha narrative is illustrated by the reaction of Gorkha majoritarian political parties to the Bengal Government's decision of forming development boards for various caste groups. In 2013, the West Bengal Government created a Development Board for the Lepchas, a sub-group in the Darjeeling hills. Thereafter, the government went on to create more caste and other sub-group based boards. The constitution of the boards was immediately opposed by the local party which saw the imminent weakening of Gorkha identity in the recognition of caste and other sub-identities through the granting of development boards. Not only was the government opposed by Gorkha groups for its "divide-and-rule" policy, but the beneficiaries of the boards were also severely criticised for their act of breaking the ranks of Gorkha unity. In the larger Nepali speaking discourse, competing and parallel identities are not granted any discursive space. Given such a stance within the Nepali speaking public sphere, it is extremely difficult for any sub-group, particularly the Scheduled Caste sub-groups, to assert a counter culture based on their identity without being seen as betrayers or sell-outs. Nancy Fraser refers to this as a conception that assumes "that a single comprehensive public sphere is always preferable to a nexus of multiple publics" (62).

The denial of space for sub-identities through an assertion of a homogenous singular community is manifested in the political sphere too where Scheduled Caste groups have been unable to voice demand for even constitutionally mandated provisions. The glaring lack of reservations for Scheduled Castes in the local autonomous body (GTA) witnessed no visible opposition politically, socially, or in the media because GTA was perceived as the result of an agitation that had been mobilised through the aggregation of smaller groups into one large Gorkha identity. Opposing any aspect of the GTA would be tantamount to defying the very narrative of a larger community identity. Interestingly, Scheduled Caste groups had, just a few years ago, opposed the proposal to implement Sixth Schedule in Darjeeling on the ground that the proposal made no provision of reservation for Scheduled Castes (Bharatiya Gorkha Parisangh 51). This opposition to the Sixth Schedule by the SC groups was again in consonance with the Gorkha civil society opposition to the proposal. The inconsistency of the SC groups in being alternately silent and vocal about reservation provision indicates that their political action is governed more by a desire to conform to a unitary Gorkha discourse than to serve group interests.

In her essay on Dalit consciousness in Nepali literature published in 2017, Kabita Lama, who teaches in the Nepali Department of Sikkim University, writes, "Although the untouchables are known by the name Dalit in India, the Nepali speaking community has not been introduced to this word" (6).[1] Surveying the Indian Nepali literature for Dalit themes, Lama does find poems by some non-dalit poets such as Bhim Dahal, Lekhnath Chettri, and Remika Thapa that oppose varna system and caste discrimination but she concludes, "Indian Nepali poems touch upon topics such as varna system, caste discrimination, untouchability, Brahmanism and express a desire for an egalitarian society. However, a Dalit discourse is yet to develop in Indian Nepali Literature. Not much interest is shown in a Dalit discourse and developing a Dalit perspective is not encouraged" (13). Lama claimed in a telephonic interview that the essay was frowned upon by some academics and writers who felt that a discourse was being sought to be created where there was none and that it would lead to needless divisions within Nepali literature and society.

Poet and publisher Raja Puniani too, in his preface to Umesh Pariyar's *Awaidha Sapna*, talks about the absence of a Dalit discourse in Indian Nepali writings and says, "Dalit writing has emerged as a very important discourse in India. It is therefore puzzling to see a discourse that finds itself in full flow in the rest of India struggling to even crawl in the literature of our hills."

Umesh Pariyar's collection of Nepali poems *Awaidha Sapna* (Illegitimate Dream) is an example of the very few but emerging and defiant dalit voices that move beyond taking pride in a distant cultural past. His poems are about the present and express anger against claims of upper caste superiority. His poem 'Ma Damai' (I am a Damai), included in the volume, castigates those who practice untouchability:

---

1. All translations, unless mentioned otherwise, are by me.

The thread wetted by my spit has sewn the trouser you wear .... The cap that adorns your head still bears the impressions of my fingers Why, then, do your Shastras still Belittle and insult my name?

The primary challenge for Dalit discourse in Indian Nepali community is the perpetuation of caste inequalities through a strategy of denial. The Dalit identity needs to negotiate its own space in relation to an assimilating society. Jane Mansbridge describes how subtle forms of control are masked in the transformation of "I" into "we" and how subordinate groups "are silenced, encouraged to keep their wants inchoate, and heard to say 'yes' when what they have said is 'no'" (127). It is through discursive contestations in the societal, political, and literary spheres that Dalit discourse can emerge in the Indian Nepali speaking society.

Works Cited

Backward Classes Welfare Department. *Mayel Lyang Lepcha Development Board.* Kolkata: Government of West Bengal, 2013.

Bhartiya Gorkha Parisangh. *People Have a Right to Know: Evidence and Report of Parliamentary Standing Committee on Extension of 6th Schedule to DGHC Area.* Bharatiya Gorkha Parisangh, 2008.

Chettri, Leknath. *Akshar Unplugged.* Aarohan Prakashan, 2015.

Dahal, Bhim. *Tesro Pahar.* Shankar Agrawal Prakashan, 2010.

Fraser, Nancy. "Rethinking the Public Sphere: A Contribution to the Critique of Actually Existing Democracy." *Social Text* (Duke University Press), no. 25/26 (1990): 56-80. Gazmer, Binay. Telephone Interview. 2 July 2019.

Guru, Gopal. "The Dalit Movements in Mainstream Sociology." In *Dalits in Modern India: Vision and Values,* edited by S.M. Michael. Vistaar, 1999.

Lama, Kabita. "Nepali Kavitama Dalit Chetana." In *Kavita Discourse,* by Kabita Lama, Maya Prakashan, 2017.

---. Telephone Interview. 2 July 2019.

Mansbridge, Jane. "Feminism and Democracy." *The American Prospect,* no. 1. Spring (1990).

Pariyar, Umesh. *Awaidha Sapna.* Chetna Shilpa Kendra, 2016.

Puniani, Raja. "Preface." In *Awaidha Sapna,* by Umesh Pariyar. Chetna Shilpa Kendra, 2016.

Sewa, Shekhar. Telephone Interview. 2 July 2019.

Sharma, Anuradha. "'They Like Our Music, Not Us': Nepali Dalits Unite to Fight Prejudice."

The Wire. March 30, 2019. the wire.in/caste/nepali-dalits-gorkha-casteism-culture (accessed June 7, 2019).

Subba, Manprasad, and Remika Thapa. *Kinaraka Awaazharu.* Upma Publication, 2008.

Sundas, Binayak. "The Darjeeling Chronicle- I am a Damai and I am Proud of it." *Facebook.*

January 29, 2015. www.facebook.com/TheDarjChron/photos/i-am-a-damai-and-i-am- proud-of-it-writes-binayak-sundasdoes-it-bother-youcan-you/499975533473566/ (accessed June 7, 2019).

6

The Partition of 1947: Khasi lives mattered too!

Sashi Teibor Laloo

The Khasi, Jaintia and Garo indigenous communities belong to the state of Meghalaya in North- East India. The hills which they inhabit were eventually categorised as the Khasi, Jaintia and Garo Hills respectively by the British Government and later adopted by the Government of India as well. It is important to note that the state of Meghalaya was conceived on 21st January 1972, until then the Khasi, Jaintia and Garo hills were all part of undivided Assam. The Khasi community, especially those that resided on the southern foothills bordering Bangladesh, was involved in brisk socio-economic and cultural relations with the people of Sylhet (Bangladesh) for centuries. Hence, in August 1947 while the rest of India awoken to the birth of an Indian Nation little did everyone know that the indigenous communities of the North-east suffered the same fate similar to Bengal and Punjab. The task of dividing the subcontinent on the basis of "religious ethnicity" was carried by the Boundary Commission under the leadership of Cyril Radcliffe. Accordingly, the socially catastrophic line dividing India, Pakistan and modern day Bangladesh came to known as the

Radcliffe Line. The Khasi community was equally affected in the creation of Bangladesh formerly known as East Pakistan. As the Partition of 1947 led to the disruptions in the Khasi lives especially those residing on the southern foothills, post-colonial studies on the region (apart from border trade and migration studies) have not formed any comprehensive study on the Khasi Hills so far.

The reason for the absence of literature or one may say "ignorance" thus far be understood when Ranajit Guha explains that historiography of Indian Nationalism have been dominated by colonial and national elites. Hence, one sees a very profound imprint of their achievements and contributions brushing aside (or in some insistences mentions them in a passing reference) the history and impacts of events on the marginalised communities. Guha further states that this writing and remembering of history "Fails to acknowledge, far less interpret, the contribution made by the people on their own, that is, independently of the elite to the making and development of this nationalism."(Guha, 2005, 3) However, as winds of curiosity and inclusiveness have begun to re-evaluate historiography in the past few decades, the event concerning the marginalised begins to surface. It was only in the recent decades, that scholars and writers are beginning to question the stereotypes that have dominated the Partition narratives, which focuses mainly on Bengal and Punjab. A major gap in these studies both globally and regionally is the absence of the Khasi experience despite the fact that the Khasi Hills formed a part of the Bengal frontier experience in 1947. Paul Thomson argues that since history is recorded from the standpoint of authority, oral history thus give a fair platform to the voiceless- the under classes, the under privileged and the defeated. "in doing so, oral history has a radical implication for the social message of history as a whole" (Thompson, 2000, 6-7).

This paper will be divided into three sections. The first will highlight the significance of socio-economic relations in the Khasi southern foothills with that of Sylhet. The second part will discuss the history of including Sylhet into the Assam Province and what effect the Sylhet Referendum had on the Khasi community. The paper will conclude by voicing out another wave of Partition Studies concerning the hardships faced by the Khasi community over the years following Independence.

History of Socio-economic relations between the Khasi southern foothills with Sylhet:

> The Khasi traded with the people of Sylhet in the plains through haats (markets). Looking back in history, the functioning of the haats came to be disrupted with the arrival of the English East India Company because of the lucrative trade commodities and the revenue generated from tax. On the attainment of the Diwani Rights in 1765 the Company's gradual forays began venturing into the Bengal borderlands especially towards Sylhet which channeled limestone, coal etc. from the hills. In the context of the Khasi Hills, the year 1772 marked the appointment of William Makepeace Thackeray, was appointed the first Collector of Sylhet in which "the Company believed that their right extended to the foothills and that the Sylhet plains which were a natural extension of the Bengal plains". (Syiemlieh 2006, 31) Even though there were political tensions between the Indigenous Chiefs and the Company in controlling the haats along the foothills, it is important to keep in mind that to the traders, trade and commerce persisted keeping aside the eventual raids and disturbances which were often resulted in punishments.

In the late 18th century, according to the reports of the Company officials, the larger and more important haats which connected the hills and plains along the southern foothills was Pandua, Punatit and Jaintiapur. (Syiemlieh, 2006,329) Coming to the 19th century trade centers further flourished. J N Chowdhury in the book Khasi Canvas observed that "Dr Lamb who arrived with his Wife and Mr. Tucker at Cherrapunji in 1828 remarked that the Khasis had close trade relations with the plains of Sylhet." (Chowdhury, 1998,254) The East Pakistan District Gazetteers also gives an account that

> From the remote past, the inhabitants of the plains of the Surma Valley had trade relations with the Hill Tribes. Tribal trade centers like Cherrapunji, Jowai, Mowphlang, Dawki, Jaflong, etc., were frequently crowded by the people of Sylhet and the Khasis in turn made profitable business at Sylhet towns and Markets. Ultimately when the Khasis found their products, especially Pan, in great demand they came down in hordes and settled in the plains where life was comparatively easier. (Rizvi, 1970, 104)
>
> The principle markets in the 20th century along the foothills hills and Sylhet were Bholagunj, Chattack, Lakhat and Jaintiapur. The markets were held at a regular interval of every eight days to enable the hill men's periodic visit to the various haats. The Syiem (Chief) of Sohra and Khyriem levied market dues at Lakhat and Bholagunj respectively. Others Syiems with land towards Sylhet also had control over the markets from which they derived Khrong, a levy. (Syiemlieh, 2008, 57)

As it was geographically more favourable for the Khasi foothills to trade with Sylhet through pathways and boats through the plentiful rivers, the main commodities exported to the plains were fruits like oranges, potatoes, Tejpat, beetle-nut, pan and various other spices. Among the abundant minerals which drew the attention of the west towards the Khasi hills were the finest qualities of limestone, coal, stone and iron. From the plains commodities like rice, salt, tobacco, fish, oil, corals, brass, copper utensils, clothes and livestock like cattle and goats went up the hills.[1] P. R. T. Gurdon goes on to say that

1. See Lieutenant H. Yule, "Notes on the Kasia Hills and People" in Journal of the Asiatic Society of Bengal, Volume XIII , Bishop's College Press, Calcutta, 1844, p. 622; A. J. M. Mills, Report on the Khasi Jaintia Hills: 1853, Assam Secretariat Printing Office, Shillong, 1901, pp. 3-4; P. R. T. Gurdon, The Khasis, Macmillan and Co., Limited, London, 1914, pp. 44-47; B. B. Kumar, "The Border Trade in North-East India: The Historical Perspective" in Gurudas Das and R.K. Purkayastha (eds.)., Border Trade: North-East India and Neighbouring Countries, Akansha Publishing House, New Delhi, 2000, p. 8; David Ludden, Investing in Nature around Sylhet: An Excursion into Geographical History, Economic and Political Weekly, Volume 38, No. 48, November 29th, 2003, p 5082; David Syiemlieh, "Control of the Foothills: Khasi-Jaintia Trade and Markets in Late Eighteenth Century" in F. A. Qadri (ed.)., Society and Economy in North-east India, Vol. 2, Regency Publications, New Delhi, 2006, p. 333.

gradually the Marwari merchants from the plains attended all the markets frequented by the hill-men and exported the goods to Calcutta. (Gurdon, 1914, 48)

Sylhet and the Referendum

For many centuries, Sylhet had depended as well as catered to the needs of the Khasi community, likewise the Khasi hills functioned as an important corridor for the flow of goods and natural resources between Sylhet and Assam in the north. The East India Company made Sylhet into a District in the year 1782 and associated it with the Province of Bengal. However, in 1878 the district of Sylhet was incorporated to the Province of Assam.

Looking into the politics that shaped the crucial years preceding the Independence of India, Binayak Dutta opines that When the Cabinet Mission arrived with the grouping plan, the Assam Congress leaders opposed the Cabinet Mission for placing Assam in Group "C" along with Bengal, but pointed out that they had no objection to the transfer of Sylhet from Assam to Bengal. When the Muslim League led by Muhammad Ali Jinnah demanded the inclusion of Assam in Pakistan, the Congress leadership rejected the idea but agreed to the referendum in Sylhet. When Lord Mountbatten announced the decision of the colonial state to organise a referendum, the Congress, the Communist and the Jamiat-ul-Ulama-i- Hind was on one side and the Muslim League and the Jamiat-i-Islami on the other, jumped into the campaign. It was this battle which decided Sylhet's fate after 14th August 1947. (Binayak, 162)

In the implementation of the "Two Nation Theory", new dominions was made concrete by the Mountbatten Plan or the 3rd June Plan, as it was the official division of British India and it was announced by Mountbatten on 3rd June 1947. Two among the agendas of the Plan mentioned above which concerning this paper was that: 1. Sylhet to be decided under a referendum and 2. A boundary commission would be set up to tackle the complexities in the formation of East and West Pakistan.

The 1946 elections had resulted in the Muslim League and its supporters winning 90% of the seats reserved for Muslims, thus, it was effectively a plebiscite where the Indian Muslims voted on the creation of separate Muslim nation called Pakistan. (Mohiuddin, 2006, 70) The referendum, also known as the Sylhet Referendum in July 1947 resulted in the people of Sylhet voting in favour of the Muslim League which permanently settled Sylhet to East Pakistan for good.

The Sylhet Referendum as one may observed was a precursor to the result given by the Boundary Commission in August 1947. Despite the presence of a thriving Khasi population in Sylhet, the only task ahead for Cyril Radcliffe and his team was to depend on the topography of the area which comprised of the hill-plain dichotomy (similar to the East India Company's initial boundary in mercantile interest) and in many instances using the rivers as a demarcating medium. It is important to understand that rivers have a character of their own, they change courses in time and they vary in size from season to seasons.

Partition Studies Concerning India's North-East

In order to understand why the Partition of 1947, permanently disabled the socio-economic relation between the foothills and the plains, one must venture into the complexities undergone in the separating the nations resulting in the chaos and displacements. One may observed the number of areas that were interdependent with Sylhet through a circular dated 26th November 1912, when the Deputy Commissioner addressed the Syiem (Chief) or "Merchant Kings"[1] of Sohra, Malai Sohmat, Bhowal, Maharam, Langrin, Nongstoin as well as the Sordars of Sohbar, Wahlong, Mawlong, Mawdon, Dwara Nongtyrnem and the Wahadadars of

1. The term "Merchant Kings" to denote the above rulers can be observed in P. N. Dutta, Relations of the Khasis and Jaintias with their Southern Neighbours till the British Intervention in Proceedings of the North East India History Association, First Session, Singhania Printing Press, Shillong, 1980 p. 76.

Shella whose lands shared a border with Sylhet.[1] Nari Rustomji who was the advisor of Tribal Areas to the Governor of Assam, clearly mentioned in his book Enchanted Frontiers (1971) that:

> In Partition days, the main market for the produce of the Khasi Hills was in the District of Sylhet skirting their Southern border. With Partition, Pakistan embarked on a virtual economic blockade of the Khasi Hills. Movement of goods between the Khasi Hills and Sylhet was discouraged... The object of the exercise was no doubt to put pressure on the Khasis and create among them a feeling that they would be better off in Pakistan. The hill people on the extreme southern borders of the Khasi hills were driven to a state of near panic. (Rustomji, 1971, 110)

The District Gazetters of East Pakistan also pointed out that "The Marwari capitalists left Sylhet for good."(Rizvi,1970, 251) Further, it was estimated that Assam lost a total of 4769 square miles of territory and a population of 28, 25,282 as a consequence of the Radcliffe Line. (Dutta, 164) With the emergence of Bangladesh, there was an attempt between India and Bangladesh to resume trade and alleviate the economy of the border areas and a few border haats were opened between December 1970 and March 1971. However, threatened with the influx of refugees into Meghalaya, the border trade sadly came to a halt. (Gassah, 1996, 180-181 and Pyrngap, 2017, 110) The Partition of 1947, especially in the context of the Khasi community needs to be understood not through the horrific decisions of the Boundary Commission alone, but through a comprehensive understanding of colonial politics in the region.

In conclusion, with the setting in of nationalism in the 20th century political boundaries were made concrete on the lines of ethnicity, religion and geography or at times a mixture of all three leaving many communities at stake. The southern foothills of Meghalaya just like the other areas that were affected, are gradually questioning the "spotlights of Partition studies" where

1. Meghalaya State Archives., Circular No. 711-21, Dated 26th November 1912.

equal academic light is necessary on all the regions who suffered the same fate as well. In the name of a modern political boundary, the Partition took for granted the Khasi community's age old traditions of a territorial space and socio-economic dependencies with the people of Sylhet. Despite the vast array of academic work done on the Partition of 1947 which was focused largely on Bengal and Punjab, the catastrophic event concerning North-eastern India has come to surface only a few decades ago and thus needs much academic attention.

Works Cited

Chowdhury, J.N. The Khasi Canvas: A Cultural and Political History, Calcutta, Jeetra Offset, 1998.

Dutta, Biyanak. "The Past as Present: Partition in Assam Politics during Independence and Beyond", New Delhi, Dialogue, Vol. 16, No. 1, 2014.

Gurdon, P. R. T. The Khasis. London, Macmillan and Co. Limited, 1914.

Gassah, L.S. "Reorganisation and the Economic Problems of the Border Areas of Jaintia Hills." Reorganisation of North East India since 1947, (eds.) B.Datta Ray and S.P. Agarwal, New Delhi, Concept Publishing Company, 1996.

Guha, Ranajit. "On Some Aspect of the Historiography of Colonial India" in Ranajit Guha (ed.), Subaltern Studies 1: Writings on South Asian History and Society, New Delhi, Oxford University Press, 2005 (reprint).

Mohiuddin, Yasmin Niaz. Pakistan-A Global Studies Handbook. California, ABC-CLIO, 2006.

Pyrngap, Lasoborki. "Partition and Economy of the War Area of Khasi and Jaintia Hills of Meghalaya. " New Delhi, Dialogue, Volume 18, No.3, 2017.

Rizvi, S. N. H. (ed). The East Pakistan District Gazzetters: Sylhet, Dacca, East Pakistan Government Press, 1970.

Rustomji, Nari. Enchanted Frontiers: Sikkim, Bhutan and India's North Eastern Borderlands. Bombay, Oxford University Press, 1971.

Syiemlieh, David R. "Control of the Foothills: Khasi-Jaintia Trade and the Markets in the Late Eighteenth Century." Society and Economy in Northeast India, in F. A. Qadri (ed.), Vol. 2, New Delhi, Regency Publications, 2006.

_______ "Trade and Markets in the Khasi Jaintia Hills: Changed Conditions in the 19th and 20th Centuries." Society and Economy in North-East India, (eds.) David R Syiemlieh and Manorama Sharma, Volume 3, New Delhi, Regency Publication, 2008.

Thompson, Paul. The Voice of the Past: Oral History. Oxford University Press, 2000 (Third Edition)

7

Patriarchal manipulation of Faith and Silencing of women in Tehmina Durrani's *Blasphemy* and Fadia Faqir's *My Name is Salma*

Ruqayya Bahar

Throughout her life, a woman is a slave at the hands of patriarchy and society at large. Her father has authority over her in childhood, her husband in youth and her son in old age. She is ever silenced by the changing male authority over her. While women are rendered speechless for various social and cultural factors, one main cause for this regression is the manipulation of religion by the patriarchal agency, existing both within the society and the private space of home. Whether a woman is five or thirty-three, men including her own father and husband can abuse or slaughter her, silencing her once and for all, and validate it by accusing the very woman for bringing such vicious fate upon herself. Here, the so called "safe" home can be an even more dangerous place. This paper seeks to analyse two such works,*Blasphemy* by the Pakistani-British writer Tehmina Durrani and *My Name is Salma* by the Jordan based novelist Fadia Faqir. Inspired by real life incidents, both Durrani and Faqir try to uncover how these male members of the family leave no stones unturned to silence the females for their own narcissistic gains. Given religion as an excuse, women are further muted by having no say in this patriarchal domain. Nevertheless, both the writers reflect upon the need of rising above this conventional silence. Neither of them present Islam in a negative light, but the consequences of misusing religion for rendering women voiceless. Both Durrani and Faqir assert progressive Islam as a way for female liberation. A collective societal effort is required to address this mission where home is the primary unit to initiate change from.

During the colonial times, one set of laws applied to almost entirely to women, and was aimed specifically at muting their voices. They could be harshly punished and humiliated simply for talking too much or too publicly or in a tone of voice that seemed grating or nagging. In patriarchal societies, women are objectified and repressed; the dominant metaphor is that of silence. Silences are complex spaces of power and resistance and it could be the intentional or imposed state of muteness.

With the intention of opening the eyes of those oppressed, this paper presents a detailed analysis on several instruments of patriarchal monopoly that uses religion as its key device of repression. How men within the family manipulate this shortcoming to relegate and control women is the major discussion in this paper. The paper also discusses how women themselves become the contributors to their own oppression believing it's wiser to remain passive and voiceless rather than speaking up only to attract insult and punishment.

The weak socio-economic status of the women handicap and leaves them at the mercy of the male members of the family, who remain insensitive to their care and development. Whether it is the campaigns to combat forced marriage in Muslim and non-Muslim Asian communities or honour killings in Arab regions and the Middle East, current efforts and management policies are certainly not enough. Since the women in the Muslim world are still traumatised by male domination and tyranny, more serious efforts need to be made to identify and help the girls and women at risk.

One cannot possibly neglect women's submission to such controlling and patriarchal attitude. They are mostly dependent on the family members who might as well be their own abusers but instead of stepping out for confrontation and legal action they choose to remain voiceless because the fear of getting rebuked instead of the actual culprit is too strong. Some women even give in and believe they have brought such fate upon themselves for their own mistakes. Usually they are not fortunate enough to know their rights and the means to device these rights for self-protection.

Women all over the world, in one way or the other have been victimized by the lust of men. Sexual violation at work or home, abduction, dowry deaths, honour death, wife bettering, sexual slavery and trafficking are to mention just a few violations the women face, which has not been given much attention in literature until the recent times. Contemporary writings by women writers resist these patriarchal discourses by asserting the individuality of a woman.

These literary writings render explicit and implicit forms of abuse targeting women. How they become victims of physical, sexual, psychological, social, cultural, and religious violence, gets reflected in writings of contemporary women authors. Such discourses by women writers very often scrutinise the politics of violence and patriarchal monopoly against women. These writings depict patriarchy and male domination at its peak, the condition of women at their worse, and religious fundamentalism at its extreme. It brings forth the easy distortion done to religion by the hypocritical and deceitful so-called religious leaders. The descriptions are awfully disturbing and the very thought that several thousands of women, even today, are subjected to this kind of a life, makes you ponder upon it for quite some time.

Narrating her own experiences of a traumatic marriage to Ghulam Mustafa Khar, a former Governor of Punjab, which Durrani describes more broadly in her other more successful novel, *My Feudal Lord*, we see a similar theme at work in *Blasphemy* too. One can see echoes of Durrani's own prolonged suffering from a disturbed marriage. Durrani is resolute that women's status can only evolve if the patriarchal mind sets are altered from the bottom up. She argues that the real power of such feudal lords, is derived from the distorted interpretation of Islam that is supported by the silence of women and the society as a whole.

In *Blasphemy* the protagonist, Heer, held dreams in her eyes to marry Ranjha, the man of her dreams. However, after her father's death, it becomes her responsibility to marry at the earliest to make way or her younger siblings and ease the burden from her mother's shoulders. Her mother gets her married to the much older Pir Sain, a man of incredible repute, who was a saint to his people but in reality, a devil of a man.

Heer narrates, in first person, a series of negative turn of events, on stepping into Pir's household, "Here, only small errors were big sins". Without any friends or access to the outside world, it is in this confined space with closed doors, that Pir time after time abuses and rapes Heer, he forces her to sleep with strange men as '*Piyari*', watch and film pornographic content with a series of other men, "An unfamiliar hand was creeping up my thigh. I strangled a scream and clutched the quilt. Pir Sain flung it off. I shut my eyes and strangled another scream". He forcibly intoxicates Heer, and several other young girls and orphans only to drug and abuse them sexually for years. Restricted within the *haveli*, the Pir women had not seen the outside world in years. In one instance Heer says, "Like me, in reality these women had no freedom. Although they could go home, their poverty imprisoned them to the Shrine so securely that even if they dared to flee, their kith and kin were trapped in their master's gripping net." Even when they step out of the *haveli*, all necessary precautions are ensured so they do not see the external world.

The *haveli,* therefore, becomes a symbol of a living hell where ghastly horrors are executed day and night in the name of God. The Pir sexually exploits women not just to pacify his satanic lust but to boost, expand and strengthen his control and authority. While Heer is molested by one of Pir's friends she feels excruciatingly miserable. Despite all this the so called servant of God still manages to preserve his holiness and sainthood unrestrained.

Durrani also discloses how absolute powerlessness drives a woman to give in into her own repression. Heer becomes an implicit companion to her husband's lust by fetching younger girls for his pleasure so as to save her own daughters from the evil eyes of their father. She swoops down to this degree in hope of gaining some of his goodwill in return. Brutalised, silenced and desensitised, the women still count on male favour as their only means of survival.

Exposing quite a few incidents of rape in her novel, Durrani puts forward the ugly reality of corrupt politics of these God-men. *Blasphemy*, as the title itself advocates something that is contrary to the religious norms. Pir Sain, who delivers the message of God to others, distorts the rules brought about by religion for his own pleasures. Heer always wonders about Pir's obedience to religious norms, but she fails to understand the religion he is practicing.

Whatever the Pir practices, is clearly not what the *Quran* teaches. No religion teaches that. But it is the tyranny and male power built on religious codes and norms which the male strata of our society interpret for its own advantage. Where Heer's predicaments are at the hands of her devil incarnate husband Pir Sain, Salma in *My Name is Salma* suffers by the agency of her barbaric brother. The struggle of these two women is like a long never ending journey only leading to their graves as the final destination.

The happenings of the narrative in *My Name is Salma* are presented in the form of episodic flashbacks. In first person narrative, the protagonist describes her brief refuge in prison and the consequent journey to Lebanon and Exeter in hope of beginning a new life. Salma, is a young Bedouin woman, "one of the girls of the village who were ripe and ready to be plucked". In consequence of getting pregnant out of wedlock, she had to flee the bullet of her brother in the name of restoring the family honour. She is threatened to be killed for committing adultery that violates strict codes of religion and traditions established by the male elite of the Arab world. She was continuously muted by the patriarchal authority of her father and brother Mahmoud. They applied their own sort of patriarchal command over her, by keeping a constant watch on her. This savage treatment is only applicable to the females and not males where Salma is not given any opportunity to either speak up or live a life on her terms. This inferiority complex is the main reason something always holds her back in searching a new identity.

While spending several years in prison she delivers a baby girl, Layla who is taken away from her instantly after birth. Thereafter, Layla's image and sorrow along with her troubled past would haunt Salma for the rest of her life. It is in Exeter, that Salma tries forming a new identity, with a new name 'Sally Asher' and a new language (English) which she fuses with Arabic. Gradually over time, she successfully gets her postgraduate degree, marries her professor, John, have a baby boy to complete the family. However, after being long silenced and unable to bear the sighs and echoes of her long lost baby girl, Salma decides to go back home to see Layla one last time. The child being another victim of the patriarchal mechanism of control, unfortunately, was also silenced in its stage of infancy itself. She was killed by her maternal uncle Mahmoud. In facing the horrors of the socio-cultural subjugation of the Bedouin society, Salma is shot dead by the end of the novel, shutting her up once and for all, "When I turned my head I felt a cold pain pierce through my forehead, there between my eyes, and then like blood in water it spread out."

Faqir raises the question of the taboos and prohibitions which have long deprived women of their most basic rights, including the right to live a normal human life. In such societies, the concept of honour is manipulated to justify actions against women within the domestic sphere to preserve the family honour. This reinforces the notion that, the family as the smallest unit in society is accountable of ensuring the fortification of such a system at large.

There is also a common misperception among people about rape that it is the fault of women who invite or instigate a man by her provocative clothes or behaviour; or because she ventured outside her already allotted limitations. It becomes quite easy for the man to lay the guilt trap on the woman who in the eyes of her society, is a sinner and deserves no mercy or even life. Hamdan, her lover who was equally responsible for this adulterous act abandons her the very moment Salma confesses she's pregnant with his child. He refuses to marry her and disappears saying she is now "damaged goods". Salma has no choice but to keep her mouth sealed knowing the dire consequence she'd have to face in the society.

We see echoes of Faqir's own experiences throughout the narrative. Just like Salma, Faqir's child was also taken away from her. After a sour marriage which ended in divorce, Faqir lost the custody of her son. We see that the traumatic encounters of Salma cannot be entirely separated from the actual sufferings of the author herself and how patriarchy would rather eliminate blood relations than give up an inch of its power to women.

The female body becomes the main site of oppression since it is defined as something that needs continuous surveillance and observation as it cannot use rational thinking. Such mind-set leads to objectification of woman's body. The primary reason if saying directly, is the male obsession and enthralment with the female figure and sexuality. Pir Sain instructs Heer to wear heavy makeup and sexually promiscuous clothes so as to entice his guests to whom she is presented as an urban prostitute. Salma was also asked to wear a short skirt and makeup in order to look presentable enough to the male customers at the hotel where she works in Exeter, despite having a decent job of collecting and cleaning glasses from the table. She says, "There were very few women customers, and they were all better covered than I was". Even Hamdan, her ex-lover, in his own words, “You are my courtesan, my slave”, believes he owns Salma’s body where he can now exercise his force and control.

In both the novels, throughout their lives both of these women characters only suffer in silence. For Salma, death is the only respite from this torment. She flees her own country and tries to start a new life but she fails till her return to her homeland only to get shot by her brother. Whereas Heer’s misery is even worse where she devotes her entire life to struggle and fulfil the insatiable lust of her tyrant husband. And after his death, his son follows the very same path where Heer still suffers for no fault of her own. Death comes to her rescue at last.

Both the writers reflect the empowerment of the female characters who grapple with their oppressive experience. Neither of them present Islam in a negative light, but the consequences of misusing religion so as to justify the patriarchal authority over women.

An emerging class of young hyper educated women who make more money than their male counterparts and who don’t “need” a husband for the reasons their mothers or grandmothers did, remain a minority, cushioned by privilege that is unavailable to most women. It is a form of denial to act shocked that “even educated” women cave in to and perpetuate patriarchal values. Even worse, it negates the right of women who have not been fortunate enough to receive an education to demand a life that is free of the injustice of misogyny. Every woman in every region and religion deserves equality and respect.

The Muted Group Theory can be applied to both these texts where women are consistently rendered speechless and ignored. It is a critical theory concerning the certain groups of people who remain powerless compared to the others. Edwin Ardener, a British anthropologist, introduced this concept in his essays, ‘Belief and the Problem of Women’ and ‘The “Problem” Revisited’, where he named the male group as ‘dominant’ group and female group as ‘muted’ group. His noted contributions in anthropology are the studies on gender and found that the studies made by many ethnographers in the society was generalised to the male population and accumulated the finding accepting only one side. The voices of the women and other unheard have been ignored and muted. The narrow perspective to the society ignoring almost half of the population affected the studies and the muted group theory brought a light into the powers of the marginalised in the society.

The muted group theory explains the cause of muteness by a certain group of population especially of that of women in the society. The theory upholds a gender perspective where the male is the dominant class. The women live with the attitude where her opinions remain muted when spoken and mostly choose to adapt with the situation. The attitudes of the male who are the bread winners are considered dominant than the women who rely on them. The age old tradition made a whole new power division in the society.

We find that much of Heer's persona i.e. her zone falls within the boundaries of Pir Sain's dominance. Her life is totally governed and eclipsed by Pir Sain's existence. Similarly, Salma's life is governed and controlled by her feudal brother even though she fled her home years ago. Through these two male characters, both the writers bring into focus the dark and corrupt lives of the predatory male members of the family who distort religious and cultural aspects of life to attain power and silence the weak. Both, Durrani and Faqir have themselves suffered at the hands of the dominant power regime and thus aware of women's horrible plight in society. It was the call of the hour to speak out, breaking the age-long silence. Durrani and Faqir through representing their lives in these novels become synecdoche, who stands for the whole.

Their life and suffering represent the very mirror of every woman who undergo such turbulent life and is unable to raise a voice.

Works Cited

Adhikary, Soumita. Autobiography as Testimony: Truth and Fiction in Tehmina Durrani's Writings". *International Journal of English Language, Literature and Humanities,* vol. 2, no. 5, September 2014, pp. 375- 381. *IJELLH.* https://ijellh.com/papers/2014/September/37-370-383-sept-2014.pdf?x72302

Alqahtani, Suaad Muhammad. "Western Feminism or Return to Authentic Islam? Jordanian Women in Faqir's Pillars of Salt and My Name is Salma". *Arab World English Journal for Translation and Literary Studies*, vol. 2, no. 7, May 2017, pp. 81- 82. *AWEJ Journal.* https://pdfs.semanticscholar.org/8963/56eb4b33a2ac2faa463182c4c823265f57b9.pdf

Aziz, Zarizana Abdul, and Moussa Janine. *The Due Diligence Principle and the Role of the State: Discrimination against Women in Family and Cultural Life.* https://www.ohchr.org/Documents/Issues/Women/WG/Family/Written_Submissions/DDP_Submission_UNWG_Discr%20ag%20Women%20Family%20Cultural%20Life15.pdf

Durrani, Tehmina. *Blasphemy*. Penguin, 1999.

Durrani, Tehmina. *My Feudal Lord.* Corgi Books, 1998.

Eltahawy, Mona. *Headscarves and Hymens: Why the Middle East Needs a Sexual Revolution.* W&N, 2016.

Faqir, Fadia. *My Name Is Salma*. Black Swan, 2010.

Khan, Sajad Ahmad. "Patriarchal Structure (Denying the Role of Women as Futile and Abstract) Violence against Women". *IOSR Journal of Humanities and Social Science*, vol. 11, no. 5, 2013, pp. 94-99. *IOSR Journals*, http://www.iosrjournals.org/iosr-jhss/papers/Vol11-issue5/P01159499.pdf

Khan, Zaynab. *Women Rights and Islam.* Linköping University, Dissertation. http://www.diva-portal.org/smash/get/diva2:20362/FULLTEXT01.pdf

Khatwani, Lata. "Surrendering Body and the Rebelling Soul: Woman, Body and Space in Tehmina Durrani's Blasphemy". *Euacademic.Org*, 2014, http://euacademic.org/UploadArticle/1102.pdf

Sarnou, Dalal. "Deterritorialized Anglophone Arab Women: Liminal Selves between Home and Diaspora (Case Study of Faqir's My Name is Salma)". *Riull. Ull.Es*, http://e-biblio.univ-mosta.dz/bitstream/handle/123456789/10784/DETERRITORIALIZED%20ANGLOPHONE%20ARAB%20WOMEN.pdf?sequence=1&isAllowed=y

Sundus, Areeba. "Book Review: 'Blasphemy: A Novel' by Tehmina Durrani". *Feminism in India*, 2018, https://feminisminindia.com/2018/10/30/blasphemy-tehmina-durrani-review/

8

The Construction of Silence and politics of with holding in MG Vassanji's *The Book of Secrets*

Somya

"History drifts about in the sands, and only the fanatically dedicated see it and recreate it, however incomplete their visions and fragile their constructs."

M. G. Vassanji, *The Book of Secrets*

The book *The Book of Secrets* contains the past and history, though in fragments, of an immigrant Indian Shamsi Muslim community in East Africa with European colonialism and African nationalism as the backdrop. The epigraph of the text is taken from The Rubaiyat of Omar Khayyam that initiates the narrative with a profound suggestion that one's past is never dead, and is always at hand in one's present or, in other words, the past forms the bedrock of the present. As such, the fragments of the history of the Indians in East Africa are contained in the personal diary of a colonial officer, Alfred Corbin, who works in East Africa during British colonialism in the region and records his keen observations in his diary which eventually falls in the hands of an Indian shopkeeper, Feroz, a former student of Pius Fernandes, a Goanese Indian, and he somehow realises its historical value and hands it over to Fernandes who undertakes to trace out the history of the diary and to elaborate the historical fragments contained in it to uncover many secrets therein. Subsequently, he recreates the past, but many questions remain unanswered, utterly unknown and unknowable lending the text a postmodern quality. The story is replete with gaps and silence and the characters stay in a sense of ambivalence or to use Homi Bhabha's words – an in betweeness or state of hybridity. Vassanji's novel builds through implication an allegorical layering where a "past" is engaged by a "present"— mirrors the colonial frontier separating the coloniser from the colonised (the white from the black or brown). In this construction, we see border skirmishes between the parallel binaries of coloniser/colonised and present/ past. From the start, the text sets up some interesting paradoxes emblematic of the society of East Africa itself where there exists no simple binary of "slave and master" but rather a three-part structure (and even this simplifies a much more heterogeneous society) of relations between the British whites, "immigrant" Indians, and the indigenous blacks.

As a postcolonial writer, Vassanji tries to deconstruct the difference between the coloniser and the colonised, dominant and dominated. He examines the lives of the migrants and immigrants: "the Indian diaspora is very important...once I went to the US, suddenly the Indian connection became very important: the sense of origins, trying to understand the roots of India that we had inside us." (Kanaganayakam, p. 21). Whereas Ngugi waThiong in his works like *A Grain of Wheat* (1967) represents the colonial binarism and hegemonic attributes of the society, Vassanji in his novels portrays the marginalised and excluded East African people who live a life of ambiguity and ambivalence. They are the continuous prey to the colonial defiance and degradation that often remind them of their marginalised and inferior race and colonial coercion. Hybridity in the lives of the characters is the outcome of their intimate contact, during their way of migration and immigration, with the people of different castes, religions, sects, creeds etc.

Vijay Mishra tends to be skeptical of the label "diaspora" being applied to anyone who considers their dislocation in happier times. He opines that the diasporic imaginary constitutes of an unhappier breed whose growing fortunes cannot really compensate for the pain that they continue to suffer of severance from their object of love, their homeland, an object which no longer exists in reality and can therefore never be regained. Vassanji's story of the British Empire in East Africa is a very postmodern mediation on the allures and pitfalls of narrative. It's set in the racial melting pot of East Africa, where African, Arab, Indian, English and German cultures mesh. In the novel, Fernandes reads the diary, talks to those who knew some of the people referred to, and offers excerpts, possible interpretations of events, as well as accounts of his own life. In his entries, Corbin records impressions of the new country and of his relations with Asian shopkeepers and local Africans, but he seems--as Fernandes will later be–most obsessed with Mariamu, a beautiful Indian African woman who becomes his servant. Mariamu is accused of being possessed; she is not a virgin when she marries Pipa, a merchant and later a spy; and Ali, the son she soon gives birth to, is suspiciously fair. The truth of Corbin's relationship with Mariamu is further complicated by Pipa's ambiguous espionage during the world war. Ali, who immigrates to Britain, eventually meets Corbin; but Fernandes, failing to learn what the truth of Ali's parentage might be, accepts the fact that perhaps we can never know the past except incompletely, "as incompletely as we know ourselves."

The Book of Secrets is a novel of the in-between. It explores the border between the self and the other, between giving voice and remaining silent, between the centre and periphery as wall between the pure and the hybrid. Its text is located at the intersection between story and history, between the fictional and the factual as well as between realism and representational character of all art. It is a "post-colonial as well as post-modern novel." M.G. Vassanji claims that his novel *The Book of Secrets* 'traces the origins of a community, its development in a British colony, and finally its dispersal in the postcolonial era' (13). In a complex and often captivating manner, Vassanji uses deeply gendered representations in tracing what he calls the origins of a community. The Book of Secrets embeds women characters in its plot structure, but can be read as a semi-autobiography of its main male narrator, Pius Fernandes, an Indian History and Literature teacher who has immigrated to Tanzania. The novel is partly commemorative, albeit in a benignly satirical way, of the silenced histories of women during East Africa's encounter with Arab traders, Indian settler communities and European colonialists. I paper will focus on Vassanji's portrayal of female characters and argue that his self-reflexivity leads to their allegorical deployment as metaphors and types for his literary and ideological projects of tracing the origins of the Indian community, its development in European colonies in East Africa, and finally its dispersal in the postcolonial era. In his use of female characters as metaphors, Vassanji's style comes very close to what Cooper suggests is 'Western writing, whose metaphors have often worked, deeply, subtly and invisibly, to caricature, conquer and colonise, through belittling the cultures it encounters' (19). Most of Vassanji's major female characters are silenced by, and metaphorically effaced from, the narrative at the very point of the excavation of their histories and at the moment of attempts to give them a voice. At these moments, allegory prevails. In other words, in reading Vassanji's novels I detect instances of what, in Loomba's words, one may call the 'feminisation of resistance'. Loomba suggests that this process limits the activity of women within nations as imagined communities (215), thereby rendering their position subaltern.

Although seemingly occupying an integral part in the structural design of the novels, female characters are largely the 'leitmotif' of Vassanji's book due to the allegorical nature of their depiction. It presents the possibility of an interracial sexual relationship (between a white colonial administrator and an Indian woman) as a topic of speculation'(189). In his use of female characters, Vassanji's ideological and literary strategy in both narratives comes very close to what Quayson calls 'symbolisation' (82). Quayson states that symbolisation is characterised by 'an insistent metaphorical register even when this register does not help to develop the character fully. In the book, Khanoum, the black wife of mukhi Jamali, the tragic Mariamu and her passionate and rebellious daughter-in-law, Rita, are both indispensable to the structural configuration of the novel. Vassanji's two novels are structurally celebrate women's subjectivity, but paradoxically lack a gender-sensitive theoretical framework of agency that would allow the women characters to become fully rounded. Both novels are narrated largely by their male protagonists who, supposedly, attempt to capitalise on the subaltern experiences of women. It is interesting that male characters such as Corbin, mukhi Jamali and even the illiterate Pipa are given spaces in which they either become narrators or at least focalisers. For example, Part One of *The Book of Secrets* titled 'The Administrator', a reference to colonial Assistant District Administrator Alfred Corbin's experiences in Kikono, could also arguably be named 'Mariamu' because these experiences are inextricable from Mariamu's presence. Mariamu is presented through the male gaze and filtered through a number of masculine colonialist tropes'. Corbin's first encounter with Kikono is his almost surreal sighting of Mariamu. The narrator reports: And this was what appeared to the new ADC as he approached the town: fleeting glimpses caught between bush and tree and anthill – a figure draped in white, dashing from left to right, cutting across his path in the distance. It could have been a man in kanzu but for the black hair flying, the lithe movement, the nimble step ... then a red head-cover over the hair to complete the female figure. So amazed was he by the sight that he had stopped to watch. She disappeared behind an incline, where he was told lay the settlement ... Soon after that apparition disappeared. (28) Vassanji's use of Corbin as the focaliser is evidently motivated by his intention to expose the patronising nature of colonial logic in which 'native women and their bodies are described in terms of the promise and the fear of the colonial land' (Loomba 151). However, one wonders whether descriptions like these do not reinforce the colonial stereotypes that they are supposedly intended to debunk.

Despite the fact that in the first half of the narrative Mariamu's silent presence is pervasive, Vassanji's use of Corbin as the focaliser disempowers Mariamu. However, some critics have praised Vassanji's portrayal of Mariamu in the above and similar instances. For example, Mount suggests that 'the description of Mariamu as an apparition is significant because it ... identifies her as a figure capable of flaunting the Shamsis's preconceived gender roles; she does what no other woman does and moves about in the background, haunting Corbin' (5). One can agree with Mount insofar as his use of the word 'figure' identifies Vassanji's use of Mariamu as a tool, an object for accomplishing certain discursive objectives. To Mount's assertion that scenes like these 'invest her with agency' (5), we could add that this is paradoxical agency for it is represented through silence.7 In the case of Mariamu, Vassanji uses silence as a literary tool. But if one considers that women have been, and still are forcibly silenced in many ways, silence becomes a disturbing strategy. This is especially so if one's intention is to recover women's voices and untold stories. In fact, Mariamu is so marginalised that whatever agency she seems to have is not inherent agency that emerges from rounded characterisation but from her deployment as a Mother-Africa figure 8 In Part Two of the novel titled 'The Father and the Son', the violated and murdered Mariamu comes back as a ghost to haunt Pipa. It may be claimed that by portraying Mariamu in this way Vassanji aptly captures the painful subaltern position of women and the debilitating voicelessness that they suffer. Admittedly, however, there are occasions in the narrative where Mariamu's subjectivity is revealed. An example is when she refuses to lower her gaze when it becomes obvious that Corbin is transgressing the customary ways of male and female etiquette. The narrator says: As [Corbin] passed she did not look at him, but turned her covered head away as modesty and custom demanded ... In a sudden mischievous move, he turned, catching her unawares, and met her eyes. She stood tall, her red pachedi having fallen on her shoulders, revealing her long thick black hair, her eyes dark and deep – vagrant with the bearing of a queen, as she refused to turn away a second time.9 (77) Vassanji uses this instance, among others, to expose the condescending colonial gaze as it encounters the indigenous female. We witness in Corbin's actions what McClintock calls the colonial desire of 'civilising' the Arab women by undressing or unveiling them (31). Another example which might be held to position Mariamu as an inquisitive subject is after she has taken on the role of Corbin's housekeeper and questions his motives for coming to Kikono. Corbin records his response in his diary: 'To help your people, I offered. She looked nonplussed. On orders from my Sultan, then. That she understood' (80). At one level, the author uses this instance to expose the prevailing condescension of colonialists, which to an extent Corbin typifies. In another instance, Mariamu is portrayed as possessing some measure of agency when she steals Corbin's diary and pen. Moreover, because she is illiterate, she keeps the books hidden and unread until their death. Mariamu's silence about her past and Ali's paternity merges the woman and the books that they steal. Mariamu like the book is a potential but inarticulate source of arcane information and subversive stories. The enigmatic ways of women and closed or hidden books is highlighted in *The Book of Secrets* in Pius Fernandes's personal notebook in which he writes: 'There are questions still unanswered ... about this girl who has made such a place for herself among us – Mariamu – who stole the Englishman's diary and like that book refused to lie buried' (293). This may be read as a celebration of women's indomitable spirit. In the epilogue of, Fernandes tells the readers that what we have been reading is 'a new book of secrets ... as incomplete as the old one' – that is, as Corbin's diary. He states that we have been reading notes and scribblings and research [that he has] 'put together for Rita' (331). He cannot publish it because Rita has sworn him to secrecy. Ritais given considerable narrative voice in the novel who not only want to bury Fernandes's research but also Corbin's diary which is in Fernandes's possession. Addressing Fernandes, Rita says: 'Let it lie, this past. The diary and the stories that surround it are now mine, to bury' (298).

Vassanji uses Mariamu's silence as a metaphor for conceptualising his historicising literary project. Like Mariamu, who refuses to speak, or Corbin's diary, which is missing information due to damage or illegibility, Vassanji seems to develop a postmodernist position that stages his stories as open ended and as having silent spaces that refuse to yield all of their secrets. This is made clear by what Fernandes, who is characterised as a writer in the novel, imagines Rita to be saying about his quest to find answers about Mariamu – 'There are questions that have no answer; we can never know the innermost secrets of any heart. Each dot is infinity, Pius, your history is surface' (297). In *The Book of Secrets*, Mariamu's characterisation becomes the primary way in which the author expresses the provisionality of any literary historical project, such as his own. Vassanji's use of Mariamu's silences as both a generic and ideological strategy. For example, upon discovering Corbin's diary in the clothes of his murdered wife, a diary which Pipa himself had wanted to steal had he not been paralysed by fear, the author makes the exuberant Pipa believe that the diary was the answer to Ali's uncertain paternity, a subject that 'Mariamu had never discussed, never acknowledged, never denied' (204). Insofar as the allegorisation of the women characters is concerned, Ashcroft argues that allegory is 'a site of historical revision' (105). For Slemon, allegory is 'a site upon which post-colonial cultures seek to contest and subvert colonialist appropriation through the production of a literary, and specifically anti-imperialist, figurative opposition or textual discourse' (11). This of course echoes Fredric Jameson's famous formulation: 'Third-world texts, even those which are seemingly private and invested with a properly libidinal dynamic necessarily project a political dimension in the form of national allegory: the story of the private individual destiny is always an allegory of the embattled situation of the public third-world culture and society' (69). In a recent interview, Vassanji argues that his characters are imbued with some complexities:

'I make no claims in my fiction. I look at characters in particular situations and they are often contradictory ... My characters also often don't think themselves as either one or other, which frustrates everybody except me, of course' (in Desai 189). He certainly makes claims for his characters, especially the female ones.

By using a female character as an allegory for Africa, Vassanji panders to traditional colonial discourses that view the land as a feminine entity to be penetrated and conquered while also subverting those discourses through the process of withholding. In the text, Mariamu's silence is ambiguous: she often uses it as a means to protect herself, but her rape and murder indicate that this voicelessness is ultimately fatal. Her demise transforms her into an idol worshipped by her husband, Pipa, foregrounding the enigmatic power of the feminine made possible only in the absence of an actual female body. Moreover, Mariamu's silences and secrets occur against the background of competing masculinities that range from the hegemonic to the disruptive. Vassanji also deconstructs gender norms by suggesting a homoerotic relationship between two of the male main characters, thus furthering the case for reading The Book of Secrets from a postcolonial feminist perspective. By exploring gender issues and colonial discourses in complex and sometimes contradictory ways, Vassanji engages with recent debates in postcolonial feminist theory and provides a subtle and even covertly feminist revision of standard narratives of female victimisation and exoticism. In turn, this allows for a reading that explores the text's undertheorised consideration of agency—one that suggests that, in this novel, agency and silence are paradoxically articulated by and through one another.

Although the text freely makes use of postmodern conventions, particularly with respect to its status as historiographic metafiction, it ultimately seeks to articulate a nuanced and politicised postcolonial vision (Ball 90-99). I would like to suggest that *The Book of Secrets* also has a subtly conveyed feminist vision, primarily articulated though the representation of the character Mariamu. Scholars who have discussed Mariamu's representation and thematic function have interpreted her primarily in the way that the colonial administrator Alfred Corbin understands her: as a beautiful and mysterious presence whose silence only serves to reinforce her mystique, or simply as a victim. Amin Malak, for instance, grants Mariamu central importance in the text by referring to her as "the novel's pivotal point" (176), but he is constrained in his interpretation by his inability to see her as anything beyond an "enchanting, enigmatic figure" who is "rescue[d]" from a "harrowing exorcism" by Corbin (176). Biljana Romić laments that Mariamu's husband Pipa "finds himself cheated out of his wife's virginity on their wedding night" (76), envisioning a woman's virginity as a discreet prize to which the appropriate man is entitled. Shane Rhodes divides the text into two halves, roughly corresponding to the "narratives belonging to its two major characters, Corbin and Fernandes" (188), thus erasing the sections belonging to Rita (Fernandes's former student and the female character with the strongest voice) and Gregory (Fernandes's fellow teacher and the only queer character in the text), and considerably obscuring Mariamu's importance. Even the novel itself sometimes explicitly relegates Mariamu to the margins, such as when the narrator Fernandes introduces his text as a narrative of "the dark, passionate secret of a simple man whose life became painfully and inextricably linked with that of an English colonial officer" (8). He goes on to note that "the ephemeral tie between them—the tragic young woman Mariamu—would become the most tenacious bond of all" (8). In these ways, critics identify Mariamu either as a silent symbol or a minor character, marginalising her central role in the novel's gendered concerns.

Mariamu comes to possess the diary apparently through theft, and if she did in fact steal the journal from Corbin, this move indicates a bid to gain some control over a narrative that threatens to obliterate her. Malak reads the supposed theft of the diary as an oppositional move when he writes, "this gesture on the part of the illiterate, silent subaltern represents a daring, subversive act that symbolically signifies a form of resistance, retrieval, and appropriation of the tools of the dominant discourse whose codes are to be deciphered a generation later" (177-78). This argument is certainly reflected on the first page of the novel when the narrator asserts that if Corbin's diary were stolen, the colonised subjects could "take back [their] souls, [their] secrets from him" (1). The only problem with this interpretation is that Malak takes the claim that Mariamu stole the diary at face value. Pipa certainly believes that Mariamu stole the diary from Corbin, but he also improbably concludes that it is her "gift" (172) to him to show that "she had chosen him over that other" (204), ironically making himself the centre of the event even though the diary was clearly hidden from him. It is true that Pipa finds the diary in Mariamu's possession after her murder, and Corbin claims many years later that it was stolen, but this evidence does not preclude the conclusion that Mariamu obtained the diary through other means (e.g., Corbin could have given it to her). How the diary wound up in Mariamu's possession opens up thorny questions of complicity, agency, and coercion. Several questions come to mind. Did she steal it? If so, why? Did she believe it contained her secrets or even her soul? Was it a self-conscious act of resistance? Was it an attempt to hide her unfaithfulness? Regardless of the answer, the recognition of Mariamu's agency is critical to a feminist reading of the text. The question of agency is a "tension both within and around postcolonial theory" (Williams and Chrisman 6). As an Indian/African woman negotiating her multiple positioning in patriarchal and colonial discourses, Mariamu possesses a sense of agency that is mediated and restricted by such institutions as the family and colonialism. Her ability to speak and be heard therefore risks being interpreted in a very limiting fashion. In the well-known essay "Can the Subaltern Speak?," Gayatri Chakravorty Spivak addresses the question of agency of those at the bottom of the social hierarchy. Considering gender along with class, Spivak concludes:

> [B]oth as object of colonialist historiography and as subject of insurgency, the ideological construction of gender keeps the male dominant. If, in the context of colonial production, the

subaltern has no history and cannot speak, the subaltern as female is even more deeply in shadow. (82-83)

Works Cited

Abizadeh, Arash. 'Does Collective Identity Presuppose an Other? On the Alleged Incoherence of Global Solidarity'. American Political Science Review 99, 2005: 45–60.

Ashcroft, Bill. Post-colonial Transformation. London: Routledge, 2001.

Busia, A. P. A. 'Silencing Sycorax: On African Colonial Discourse and the Unvoiced Female'. Cultural Critique 14, 1989–1990: 81–104.

Conrad, Joseph. Heart of Darkness. Harmondsworth: Penguin, 1975.

Cooper, Brenda. A New Generation of African Writers: Migration Material Culture and Language. Woodbridge, UK: James Currey, 2008.

Desai, Gaurav. 'Ambiguity is the Driving Force or the Nuclear reaction Behind my Creativity: An E-Conversation with M.G. Vassanji'. Research in African Literatures 42.3, 2011: 187–197.

Eagleton, Terry. Figures of Dissent: Critical Essays on Fish, Spivak, Zizek and others. London: Verso, 2003.

Genette, G. Figures III. Paris: Seuil, 1972.

Gill, S.S. 'Politics of Location: Locating Home in M.G. Vassanji's the Gunny Sack'. Journal of Literature, Culture and Media Studies 2.4, 2010: 231–238.

Huddart, David. 'Making an Example of Spivak'. Angelaki: Journal of Theoretical Humanities 6, 2001: 35–36.

Jameson, Fredric. 'Third-World Literature in the Era of Multinational Capitalism'. Social Text 15, 1986: 65–88.

Loomba, Ania. Colonialism/Postcolonialism. London: Routledge, 1998.

Malak, Amin. 'Ambivalent Affiliations and the Postcolonial Condition: The Fiction of M.G. Vassanji'. World Literature Today 67.2, 1993: 277–282.

Marnette, Sophie. 'The French théorie de l'énonciation and the Study of Speech and Thought Presentation'. Language and Literature 10.3, 2001: 243–262.

McClintock, Anne. Imperial Leather: Race, Gender and Sexuality in the Colonial Context. New York: Routledge, 1995.

Mohapatra, A. K. 'The Paradox of Return: Origins, Home and Identity in M.G.Vassanji's The Gunny Sack'. Postcolonial Text 2.4, 2006: 1–21.

Mount, Durant. 'Dealing with Another Culture's Ghosts: Mariamu, Diaspora and Contact Zones in M. G. Vassanji's The Book of Secrets'. Postcolonial Text 5.4, 2009: 1–15.

Naaman, D. 'Woman/Nation: A Postcolonial Look at Female Subjectivity'. Quarterly Review of Film and Video 17.4, 2000: 333–344.

Nfah-Abbenyi, J.M. Gender in African Women's Writing: Identity, Sexuality, and Difference. Bloomington and Indianapolis: Indiana University Press, 1997.

Parry, Benita. 'Problems in Current Theories of Colonial Discourse'. Oxford Literary Review 9, 1987: 27–58.

Prakash, Gyan. 'Subaltern Studies as Postcolonial Criticism'. The American Historical Review 99.5, 1994: 1475–1490.

Quayson, Ato. Calibrations: Reading for the Social. Minneapolis: University of Minnesota Press, 2003. 11 November 2013 97 Gender, the Subaltern and the 'Construction of Silence.'

Quayson, Ato. 'Symbolization: Testing a Psychoanalytical Category on Postcolonial African Literature'. University of Toronto Quarterly 73.2, 2004: 754–772.

Rimmon-Kenan, Shlomith. Narrative Fiction. London: Methuen, 1983. Simatei, Tirop. P. The Novel and the Politics of Nation Building in East Africa. Germany: Bayreuth African Studies 55, 2001. 82.

Slemon, Stephen. 'Post-Colonial Allegory and the Transformation of History'. Journal of Commonwealth Literature 23.1, 1988: 157–68.

Spivak, C. Gayatri. In Other Worlds: Essays in Cultural Politics. New York: Methuen, 1987.

—. 'Can the Subaltern Speak'. Marxism and the Interpretation of Culture. Ed. C. Nelson and L. Grossberg. Basingstoke: Macmillan Education, 1988a: 247–313.

—'Political Economy of Women as Seen by Literary Critic'. Coming to Terms. Ed. E. Weed London and New York: Routledge, 1990.

—. A Critique of Postcolonial Reason: Toward A History of the Vanishing Present. Cambridge, Massachusetts and London: Harvard University Press, 1999.

Stratton, Florence. '"Periodic Embodiments": a Ubiquitous Trope in African Men's Writing'. Research in African Literatures. 20.1, 1990: 111–26.

Toron, Alison. 'Refusing to Tell: Gender, Postcolonialism, and Withholding in M.G. Vassanji's The Book of Secrets'. Postcolonial Text 5.3, 2009: 1–15.

Vassanji, M.G. The Book of Secrets. London: Picador, 1996 [1994].

Weber, Eugen J. Peasants into Frenchmen: The Modernisation of Rural France, 1870–1914. Stanford: Stanford University Press, 1976.

9

Pervading yet Subversive Silence in Arundhati Roy's novel *The Ministry of Utmost Happiness*

Anjali Dawar

Introduction: George Eliot makes a poignant point in *Middlemarch*:

> "If we had a keen vision and feeling of all ordinary human life, it would be like hearing the grass grow and the squirrel's heart beat, and we should die of that roar which lies on the other side of silence. As it is, the quickest of us walk about well wadded with stupidity."

While silencing has been a weapon at the disposal of the powerful, silence has been a tool in the hands of the ones oppressed too. Indubitably violence is inherent in the act of muffling another's voice and stealing someone else's agency. Silence in and of itself is not a violent act but when it is enforced and imposed upon them there is no other name for it. Indian fiction produced in English has dealt with the theme of silence time and time again. Shashi Deshpande's novel *That Long Silence* and the novel

Fire on the Mountain by Anita Desai are some texts that testify to this in varying measure.

This essay is entitled "Pervading Yet Subversive Silence in Arundhati Roy's Novel *The Ministry of Utmost Happiness*" Spanning the 1950s to the 2010s, the 2017 novel is Eliotesque (George Eliot) in scope and Rushdiesque in style. One meets several characters and comes across variegated plots and sub-plots. The novel is enmeshed in several interconnected strands and stories. It traverses back and forth in time. But the two characters who emblematise and echo the present theme are Anjum and Tilottama. The tale of the former is set in Delhi and that of the latter is located in Kashmir. The Atlantic states:

> "It tours India's fault lines, as Roy has, from the brutal suppression of tribal populations to the 2002 pogrom against Muslims in Gujarat… Just about every resistance movement is embodied in a character, and the lives and struggles of these characters intersect. The queers, addicts, Muslims, orphans, and other casualties of the national project of making India great again find one another and form a raucous community of sorts. And this novel—this fable—is as much for them as about them; it commemorates their struggles and their triumphs, however tiny."

The subaltern in this novel has a voice and agency. And existence of the powerless is not portrayed as entirely meaningless. The private, inner circle lends layered gravity and cadence to the silent sufferers too.

ANJUM: The novel begins with the ominous sentence: "She lived in the graveyard." The "She" is Anjum. Free-flowing and unabashed conversations take place at this point in the story. However, as one slips into history a more virulent and suffocating silence bursts at the seams. One learns that Anjum, a Shia Muslim born intersex and named Aftab, was initially raised as a boy. To be born a transgender in a conventional Indian household is still considered a blow and tragedy beyond repair. When Anjum's mother, Jahanara Begum, discovers "girl parts" in her otherwise-perfect just-born boy's body, she is shattered.

> "In Urdu, the only language she knew, all things, not just living things but *all* things – carpets, clothes, books, pens, musical instruments – had a gender. Everything was either masculine or feminine, man or woman. Everything except her baby. Yes of course she knew there was a word for those like him – *Hijra.* Two words actually, *Hijra* and *Kinnar.* But two words do not make a language."

The narrator's comment right after this thought runs like this:

> "Was it possible to live outside the language? Naturally this question did not address itself to her in words, or as a single lucid sentence. It addressed itself to her as a soundless, embryonic howl."

Mulaqat Ali, a *hakim* by profession and Aftab's (the name Anjum is accorded by her parents) well-meaning father tries everything including surgery to fix his son. But one day when Aftab witnesses a "tall woman with lipstick, gold high heels and a shiny, green satin salwar kameez," he irrevocably leaves the heteronormative mantle behind to cloak in the god-given trans identity. Aftab enters Khawabgah. This is where he grows up from teenage years well into his 40s. Thus, begins a relatively un-silent part of Anjum's life. The day Aftab is allowed in for the first time, his elation is palpable:

"It was the only place in his world where he felt the air made way for him."

Khawabgah is a place populated by the fringe, the outsiders and the misfits. They refer to the conventional as *duniya.* The idea of Othering as explained by Edward Said is turned on its head and roles are reversed repeatedly in the course of the novel. Nimmo, one of the residents asks Aftab if he knew why God made Hijras? He did not and she fills in the gaps:

> "It was an experiment. He decided to create something, a living creature that is incapable of happiness....think about it, what are the things that you normal people get unhappy

> about? … for us the price-rise and school admissions and beating-husbands and cheating wives are all *inside* us. The riot is *inside* us. The war is *inside* us. Indo-Pak is *inside* us. It will never settle down. *It can't.*"

Unable to comprehend this unsettling picture, at fourteen Aftab finally does grasp Nimmo's morbid interpretation. As his body metamorphoses into a masculine form outside and still feminine inside and as his once-sweet voice loses the charm he chooses to resort to silence unfamiliar to him just yet.

> "He was repelled by it and scared each time he spoke. He grew quiet, and would speak only as a last resort…He stopped singing."

Clearly silence doesn't dawn only when extrinsically forced, it is a warped living breathing thing that takes hold from within too. Once music left Aftab he departs from *duniya* for good and enters Khwabgah as a permanent resident.

On Anjum's eighteenth birthday Ustad Kulsoom Bi, one of the chiefs of the Delhi Hijra Gharana, trows her a party. Bedecked in a "red 'disco' sari", with a backless choli, Anjum goes to bed imagining herself a new bride. But her body, once again refusing definitions, confounds her.

> "She awoke distressed to find her sexual pleasure had expressed itself into her new garment like a man's."

Words are insufficient for this embarrassment. She sits in the courtyard howling like a wolf. Another way of defining oneself emerges. Ustad Kulsoom Bi, rejecting Nimmo's assessment of a Hijra, says:

> "*Hijras* were chosen people, beloved of the Almighty. The word *Hijra*, she said, meant, a Body in which a Holy Soul lives."

There is fluidity in what ones identity and no outsider gets to determine the worth and the meaning of it. Time flies haltingly and Roy gives us a candid description of how the so-called dream world is full of politics and collusions. Time plays it's role and

Anjum turns forty-six when she has the urge to adopt and rejoin the *duniya*. It's Zainab, the unwanted baby girl she found on the steps of the Jama Masjid, that spurs this desire. Anjum's approach is always personal and intimate, the external socio-political context is hardly ever the focus. *Duniya* is engulfed at various points in time in Emergency, September 11, rise of the Right-wing politics, Anna Hazare movement, Kashmir issue, Naxalite movement. But in Khwabgah sound and silence of the private prevail.

So, what happens when this unreal world of dreams and the real outside *duniya* come face to face? Anjum, accompanied by one Zakir Mian decides to go to Ajmer for a pilgrimage, as travelling alone would cause "harassment and humiliation of being seen as well as of being *unseen*." Zakir Mian, not only a man in his seventies unembarrassed to be seen travelling with a *Hijra* but also one to have once been obligated by Anjum's father, has some business in Ahmedabad too. The trip to Godhra changes Anjum's reality forever. Upon her return her silence is more disturbing than ever before. The real trumps the unreal.

"She was quiet, disconcertingly so, and spent most of her time with her books."

In fact she had been spared by the mob because of her anatomy and not their humanity. It would have spelt bad luck for them to murder and maim a *Hijra*. But the Hindu mob does not leave without throwing ridicule and expletives at her:

> "*Ai Hai! Saali Randi Hijra!* Sister-fucking Whore *Hijra*. Sister-fucking Muslim Whore *Hijra*!

Unable to ever shake off this violation and humillation, Anjum leaves the fringe for a step further-away from the *duniya*. She makes the graveyard her home where her family is buried. This works as an intense metaphor. While *duniya* cannot accommodate disparate identities, even those who are a part of the rejected fulcrum of humanity cannot always offer sanctuary or solace. Anjum has to find solace among apparitions to make any real sense of her existence.

> "For months Anjum lived in the graveyard. A ravaged, feral spectre, out-haunting every resident djinn and spirit, ambushing bereaved families who came to bury their dead with a grief so wild, so untethered, that it clean outstripped theirs."

Over time Anjum's path crosses other broken republics. Let's shine some light on Dayachand in particular. He is a Dalit converted to Islam. Vowing to kill a policeman, he acquires the name Saddam Hussain. Sehrawat, the corrupt cop is his nemesis as he had done nothing to prevent his father's lynching at the hands of frenzied *gaurakshaks*. Once again the really significant sentiments can find voice either in a whisper or complete lull.

"I was part of the mob that killed my father."

The chapter titled "Khwabgah" ends with these lines:

"Anjum wanted to die.
Saddam wanted to kill.

And miles away, in a troubled forest, a baby waited to be born."

The baby referred here is named Udaya. She is also called Miss Jebeen the Second who is birthed by Comrade Revathy, a Maoist from Andhra Pradesh who is raped and tortured by policemen. The appearance of the child is cloaked in stark silence. Anjum finds herself in a fete of sorts of fates at Jantar Mantar where several protesters and justice-seekers congregate. In the middle of this melee she sees this spectacle:

> "Her skin was blue-black, sleek as a baby seal's. She was wide awake, but perfectly **quiet**, unusual for someone so tiny. Perhaps, in those first short months of her life, she had already learned that tears, *her* tears at least, were futile."

This quiet bundle is what unites and ties all the main characters of the novel together, in solemn silence of course. Tilottama also arrives at the Hazare agitation and rescues the foundling.

TILOTTAMA OR TILO

Arundhati Roy, in an interview with Democracy Now!, an

audience-supported independent news programme, was asked if Tilo was a reflection of her own self. Roy's response was this:

> "Well, actually, to me, Tilo, Tilottama, is the fictional child of Ammu and Velutha in The *God of Small Things*, had their story ended differently. She's the younger sibling of Esthappen and Rahel. So, you know, I know her well, but I'm not her.

One does suspect though that there is a continuation of character growth of Radha, the outspoken architect that one saw in "In Which Annie Gives It Those Ones." This was a 1988 film which Roy co-wrote and acted in. With the following words Radha opens presentation of her final thesis to the jury:

> "Every Indian city consists of a 'City' and a 'Non-city'. And they are at war with one another. The city consists of a number of institutions, houses, offices, shops, roads, sewage systems ... These institutions are designed by the architect-engineer. The non-citizen has no institutions. He lives and works in the gaps between institutions, he shits on top of the sewage system."

In the same interview Roy comments on Tilo's character thus:

> "Tilo, in the book, is called the city—a country who lives in her own skin, a country with no consulates, a person whose quietness destabilises people, you know, a person whose most intimate—whose signs of being intimate with someone is to not greet them or, you know, to not change her expression when someone she loves comes."

She has three men in her life - Tilo becomes friends with three men - Musa, Naga and Garson Hobart. And they all play a convoluted role in her life. Musa is her one true love. But in a world ridden with pitfalls and landmines the coming-together is just wishful thinking. Musa is a reluctant fundamentalist. He marries Arifa and fathers Miss Jebeen the First. The little girl and her mother succumb to the same bullet. The silence of the shroud is after all most deafening.

A journalist who is based in Kashmir. Tilo marries Naga as suggested by Musa for strategic reasons and later abandons him. Kashmir context is conveyed not from the freedom fighters' perspective but through the eyes of soldiers and policemen placed there. Garson Hobart is the only character allowed a first-person perspective. He works as deputy head of the Intelligence Bureau in Kashmir. Not unike Roy's critics he complains about "grumbling intellectuals and professional dissenters who constantly carp about this great country". Garson is by no means a caricature as he understands the wrongness of what is going on in Kashmir, he is just not able to face up to his own complicity. He is infatuated with Tilo whom he is politically opposed to looks out for just the same.

Garson's colleague Amrik Singh is less lucky. In Kashmir, he runs an official torture chamber of sorts. Silence cannot be more unnerving than in a space where sadism and insanity rein king. But as irony would have it he seeks asylum in the US claiming to be a victim of torture. By the by he goes insane, kills his family and commits suicide because he cannot cope with the guilt.

In the middle of this violence and loathing Udaya alias Miss Jebeen the Second emerges as a slight ray of new possibilities. Along with Anjum and her entourage Tilo ends up in the Jannat Guest House (the graveyard). After Musa's death, the narrator tells us:

> "Tilo would grieve deeply at Musa's passing, but would not be undone by her grief because she was able to write to him regularly and visit him often enough through the crack in the door that the battered angels in the graveyard held open (illegally) for her."

Conclusion

The Telegraph has a balanced take on the book:

> "Whether it is villagers displaced by dams, or Muslims killed in the Gujarat pogrom of 2002, the still invidious caste system, or the ongoing morass in Kashmir, **she has sought to be a megaphone for the voiceless** – even if she has, at times, gone too far with her attacks on the Indian state, or been too fair to the Maoist rebels and jihadists who oppose it."

Works Cited

Eliot, George. *Middlemarch.* Wordsworth Classics, 1994.

Roy, Arundhati. *The Ministry of Utmost Happiness.* Penguin, 2017.

Roy, Arundhati. *In Which Annie Gives It Those Ones: the Original Screenplay.* Penguin Books, 2003.

Roy, Arundhati. The God of Small Things. Penguin India, 2002.

Srinivas, M. N. *Caste: It's Twentieth Century Avatar.* Penguin Books, 1996.

"Arundhati Roy on Kashmir, the Danger of U.S. Attacking Iran & Her New Book *My Seditious Heart.*" *Democracy Now!* 13th May 2019, https://www.youtube.com/watch?v=_ML6gj4KfYg.

Rahim, Sameer. "Arundhati Roy's *The Ministry of Utmost Happiness* was worth the 20-year wait." 3rd June 2017, https://www.telegraph.co.uk/books/what-to-read/arundhati-roys-ministry-utmost-happiness-worth-20-year-wait/.

10

"We could face each other over coffee cups in total silence": Analyzing Naoko in Haruki Murakami's Norwegian Wood

Chaandreyi Mukherjee

> Both in scholarly and in everyday parlance, 'memory' may refer either to the mind's general systems for the retention and retrieval of data derived from past experience, or to the specific data that are thus retrieved; either to the general awareness an individual may have of having a past dimension to his or her existence (what the philosopher Michael Oakeshott called 'a remembered past'), or to the more detailed recollection he or she may have of particular past experiences... (Cubitt 67)

Haruki Murakami's Norwegian Wood begins within this premise of memory and its various implications. The novel primarily conceived in the simplistic framework of a love story nevertheless takes shape through the dimensions of individual memory. What makes this particular novel so different from the earlier Murakami novels is the specific tone, setting and structure which venture to project it as a modest story of love, loss and subsequent maturity. Jay Rubin talks about Murakami's preoccupations while composing this novel:

> I next wrote a straight boy-meets-girl story called Norwegian Wood after The Beatles' tune. Many of my readers thought that Norwegian Wood was a retreat for me, a betrayal of what my works had stood for until then. For me, personally, however, it was just the opposite: it was an adventure, a challenge. I had never written that kind of straight, simple story, and I wanted to test myself. (150)

In Norwegian Wood, memory is afforded the primary space on which events and characters are unfolded. The novel deliberately reads like an autobiographical account emphasising elementary details of lived life. Most readers are under this impression that the male protagonist is in fact a fictional version of Murakami himself. To counter this popular idea, Murakami in one of his lectures said:

> I set Norwegian Wood in the late 1960s. I borrowed the details of the protagonist's college environment and daily life from those of my own college days. As a result, many people think it is an autobiographical novel, but in fact it is not autobiographical at all. My own youth was far less dramatic, far more boring than his. If I had written the literal truth of my own life, this two- volume novel would have been no more than 15 pages long. (Rubin 150)

The essential idea which this quote seems to project is the juxtaposition of the "literal truth" Murakami talks about with the simulated truth of the novel. Moving away from surrealism to realism, Murakami brings in minute details and concrete descriptions of everyday life in Japan. The autobiographical tone of the novel is especially associated with the predominant role ascribed to memory. The way Murakami, the author, remembers his college days and youth, is almost similar to the way the male narrator, Toru, describes his. The frailty of the human mind along with the fear of losing the memories permanently compels Toru to attempt a narration. What prompts this sudden effort at articulation is the rendition of the instrumental version of the favourite song of his beloved on a flight. This unconscious revival of memory associated with a particular person and a particular time which lay suppressed and almost forgotten in Toru's psyche proves to be the initial step in the narration of his story. He writes:

> There is no way around it: my memory is growing ever more distant... Which is why I'm writing this book. To think. To understand. It just happens to be the way I'm made. I have to write things down to feel I fully comprehend them... Writing from memory like this, I often feel a pang of dread. What if I've forgotten the most important thing? What if somewhere inside me there is a dark limbo where all the truly important memories are heaped and slowly turning into mud?... Clutching these faded, fading, imperfect memories to my breast, I go on writing this book with all the desperate intensity of a starving man sucking on bones. (Murakami 10)

Writing from memory is, thus, is provided the primary purpose of comprehending the events of the past. Writing and the narration associated with it paves a way for the clarification of semi-forgotten experiences. Memory not only provides the basic framework for the novel but is elementary in the introduction of two of major female characters, Naoko and Midori.

"I want you always to remember me. Will you remember that I existed, and that I stood next to you here like this?" (Murakami 9).

Naoko of Norwegian Wood is the fulcrum between traumatic personal past and conflicted present who with her insistence on being remembered provides the necessary impetus to the narrator to tell the story. The above quote by Naoko is interesting because it combines the idea of existence with remembrance. Memory and in this case, subjective memory, is being persuaded to formulate the idea of being. As mentioned earlier, the entire Norwegian Wood can be construed as a literary flashback which begins with a scene on a meadow with Naoko and Toru as the primary characters.

This initial chapter is significant because of the subtle hints of the predominant themes of the novel, namely love, relationship, pain, isolation and death, all threaded into the inescapable web of memory. Naoko is introduced as an emotionally vulnerable, disturbed character who is unable to imagine a blissful future with Toru who is irrefutably in love with her. The beautiful airy open meadow symbolises the hopefulness of Toru which is opposed by the claustrophobia and eventual death of deep wells which shows the pessimism of Naoko. Naoko of this novel brings into mind the earlier Naokos of Pinball, 1973 or of the short story Blind Willow, Sleeping Woman, both associated with disease, depression and eventual suicide. Toru, the narrator, clarifies, how in the past he had repeatedly failed to produce words to effectively record these memories which were undeniably more precise then. He believes the precision was primarily the problem; something which halted his role of a narrator:

> Everything was too sharp and clear, so that I could never tell where to start- the way a map that shows too much can sometimes be useless. Now, though, I realise that all I can place in this imperfect vessel of writing are imperfect memories and imperfect thoughts. The more the memories of Naoko inside me fade, the more deeply I am able to understand her. (Murakami 10)

Toru could only properly assume the role of a narrator when the memories of his past have faded. Only with the semi-erasure of his personal history can he attempt to present his story.

Despite Naoko's constant efforts she is unable to coordinate harmoniously with the social reality. She unintentionally distances herself from society and eventually from Toru. Murakami Fuminobu associates the "collapse of self-identity" linked to schizophrenia to Naoko's inability to articulate. She says, "I can never say what I want to say...I try to say something but all I get are the wrong words...or the exact opposite words from what I mean. I try to correct myself, and that only makes it worse..." (Murakami 25).

Later on, Naoko's roommate in the sanatorium informs Toru that she has started hearing voices which interferes with her composing of letters. Her schizoid self is haunted by the very real memory of her dead boyfriend and paralyses her functioning as a normal human being.

While bridging the gaps in memory, Toru narrates that Naoko was never much talkative, in fact, it was Kizuki who continued the conversation and made the environment amicable. Naoko's female voice was drowned by the talkative Kizuki when he was alive and after his death, it is the so called "good listener" Toru who insists on having "a good long talk" with her and writes so in every letter he addresses to her. It is only on the night of her birthday that Naoko launches on a talking spree. Toru notes on several occasions, "Naoko was unusually talkative that night" (48), "she had been talking non-stop for more than four hours" (49) and finally, "I thought I had better let her talk herself out" (49). Naoko's warped stories fusing into one another are portrayed as a defence mechanism where she artfully avoids any mention of Kizuki. Naoko is caught oscillating between silence and incomprehensible and redundant prattle. She becomes as Irigaray says, "spoken more than speaking, enunciated more than enunciating, the demented person is therefore no longer really an active subject of the enunciation..." (Moi 126). Naoko's power of expression is completely abolished by the world imagined by Toru in his narrative. It should be noted that it is in fact Toru's individual memory which has given expression to Naoko. In this particular domain expression itself, both spoken and written is seen as an essentially male activity. While Naoko struggles to pen a line, to think straight and to speak coherently, Toru writes one fine letter after another, with detailed descriptions of his daily life and other irrelevant details. Reiko informs Toru that his letters are beneficial to Naoko and he should not stop sending them. It seems that Murakami hints that Toru's letters and his overwhelming ability to express provides not only the sanity but a voice and identity to the "demented" Naoko.

Janet Sayers paraphrases Freud:

> ...whereas grief is triggered by actual loss of one's loved objects, depression is triggered by the experience of disappointment unconsciously as entailing loss of one's loved objects. It is this unconscious loss that causes the unhappiness of depression... Unlike grief, though, depression is much more often marked by guilt and self- accusation...Instead of addressing their anger against the external an actual causes of their unhappiness, people respond in depression by turning this anger against themselves, against their loved objects psychically internalised as phantoms within the self. It is this shadow boxing...that constitutes the stuff of self-accusations and suicidal self-destructiveness of depression. (140)

In letters and in person Naoko repeatedly tells Toru "You are not the one who hurt me. I myself am the one who did that. This is truly how I feel" (56), that she is damaged and "all kind of weird and twisted and drowning" (186). Naoko who has been doubly affected by great and terrifying personal losses and both seemingly unreasonable suicides, first of her brilliant sister and second of her love, turns the anger and frustration into herself. She is perpetually pessimistic, "But I might never recover" (193) and she feels herself to be a "burden" (115) and a "flawed human being" (116). The shadow phantoms of her self materialise as Kizuki and call her again and again to join him in death. Kizuki's death transforms Naoko into an empty shell for whom every single day becomes a battle for survival. Speaking about Kizuki she tells Toru:

> ...where our egos were concerned, the way we absorbed and shared each other's, we had no strong awareness of them... We couldn't bear to be apart. So if Kizuki had lived, I'm sure we would have been together, loving each other, and gradually growing unhappy... Because we would have had to pay the world back what we owed it... The pain of growing up. We didn't pay when we should have, so now the bills are due. (Murakami 168/170)

Naoko's relationship with Kizuki and her subsequent psychosis after his death can also be analyzed through Lacan's hypothesis of the Imaginary and the Symbolic Order where the former is the phase where the child imagines herself to have the same existence as her mother and the disruption of this phase initiates her entry into the Symbolic Order. This entry is an eventual and unstoppable phenomenon; however, problematic it might seem to the child. According to Lacan, resisting this process in order to remain in the former phase inevitably leads to social alienation and different degrees of psychosis. As Naoko's own statement quoted above suggests, she believed there was no difference between her identity and Kizuki's; they were like mother and child. J.P. Dil speaks about Jung's "pueraeternus" or eternal child and comments:

> It is a kind of Peter Pan syndrome where the temptation of staying in the womb replaces the need for individuation and adult responsibilities. Opting for this deceptively risk-free existence, however, entails its own risks. As Robert Segal explains, "To live as a puer ... is to live as a psychological infant and, ultimately, as a foetus. The life of a puer in myth invariably ends in premature death, which psychologically means the death of the ego and a return to the womb-like unconscious." (Dil 142/143)

Naoko and Kizuki were like these "eternal children", her self was replicated in Kizuki's, their egos were merged. However, this misleadingly innocent life finally brought in its own share of adult "risks" as this pristine state could not be ceaseless. Society intruded with the death of Kizuki and Naoko was brought into the realm of the Symbolic. She, however, was unable to exist in this order of things, but as per Lacanian theory she like every other person, had no choice. Despite the stringency, however, she ventured to return to the Imaginary, thereby becoming unfit to live in society.

Suicide as a familiar motif in Murakami's fiction brings into mind the rising number of suicides and various attempts over the last decade in Japan. "Japan has the 8th highest suicide rate in the world with 27,766 deaths accounted for in 2012 (The Japan

Times)" (Teixeira 1). Naoko's silence and fragmented speech becomes a tool in the hands of Murakami to explore the glaring reality of suicides related to mental illness in Japan. Silence, thus, is transformed into an expression on continuous inescapable trauma. Murakami's Naoko becomes a prototype of the vulnerable youth of Japan.

Works Cited

Cubitt, Geoffrey. History and Memory. Manchester and New York: Manchester University Press, 2007. Print.

Dil, J.P. "Murakami Haruki And The Search For Self-Therapy." Diss. http://ir.canterbury.ac.nz/bitstream/10092/1004/1/thesis_fulltext.pdf. University of Canterbury. 2007. Web. 24 January 2013.

Moi, Toril. Sexual/Textual Politics. 2nd ed. London and New York: Routledge, 2002. Print.

Murakami, Haruki. Norwegian Wood. Trans. Jay Rubin. London: Vintage Books, 2003. Print.

Rubin, Jay. Haruki Murakami and the Music of Words. London: Vintage Books, 2012. Print.

Sayers, Janet. Sexual Contradictions: Psychology, Psychoanalysis, and Feminism. London and New York: Tavistock Publications, 1986. Print.

Teixeira, Pedro Manço. "The Portrayal of Suicide in Postmodern Japanese Literature and Popular Culture Media." University of Vermont. 2014. UVM Honors College Senior Theses.Paper 15. http://scholarworks.uvm.edu/hcoltheses.

11

Silence on the Subalterns and Marginalised in Partition stories of Manto

Dr Prerana Sinha

Referring to literary genres in the 20th century, Brecht while opposing Lukacs's concept of realism, said that he would like to extend its scope. He said,[1]

> our concept of realism must be wide and political, sovereign over all conventions.... we must not derive realism as such from particular existing works, but we shall use every means, old and new, tried and untried, derived from art and derived elsewhere, to render reality to men in a form they can master.

Brecht underlines a very relevant postmodern stance as envisioned by Paul de Mann, a prominent advocate of Deconstruction in 1960s and 70s. He said a reading always reveals how the meaning of a literary text is not stable or transparent, but is radically indeterminate, and therefore it is open to further questioning.[2]

---

1. Brecht, Bertolt, **The Author as Producer**, *Eagleton's Marxismand Literary Criticism*, Routledge, 2017, p. 67.
2. Gayatri Chakraborty Spivak, *The Politics of Deconstruction* **Why** *Spivak*? Routledge Critical Thinkers, London and New York, 2003, p. 4.

Gayatri Chakraborty Spivak is critical about the lack of consideration given to the vast majority of world's population which lay in a state of abject poverty and oppression. Spivak's concern is for the subaltern women who will be silenced and contained within the technical vocabulary of western critical theory.[1]

Sadat Hasan Manto indisputably remains as one of the most powerful voices of our time: while early commentary on Partition Literature remains documented rather than representing the violence, after 1980s the focus has gone on to rewrite the history from the margins revisionist historians like Gyanendra Pandey, Urvashi Butalia, Ritu Menon and Kamla Bhasin, who have repeatedly emphasised the centrality of narratives, testimonies, eyewitness accounts, literary narratives and the role of memory while the story of the post-independence India years is irrevocably of fragmentation, relentless religious intolerance and deep disillusionment.

In her essay Leela Gandhi suggests, if independence narrated the triumphant progress of the national movement, its double, Partition, told an altogether different story—of mutual betrayal, failure, the systematic rift between Congress and the Muslim League, and the estrangement between Muslims and Hindus."[2] The story of resultant divide between Hindus and Muslims, through political wrangling escalating into the proposal to partition the Indian subcontinent on religious grounds into the independent nations of India and Pakistan, eventually witnessed one of the most horrific genocides chronicled in human history.

Priyamvada Gopal points out:[3]

> Over ten million ordinary people—Sikhs, Hindus and Muslims were dislocated from their homes and became refugees, at

---

1. *Ibid,* p. 7.
2. Gandhi, Leela, *"Novelists of the 1930s and 1940s." An Illustrated History of Indian Literature in English,* ed Arvind Krishna Mehrotra, Delhi; Permanent Black, 2003: 168-192. Print, ***Re-imagining the Nation,*** *Post-colonial Literatures,* edited by Parama Sarkar, Orient Blackswan Private Limited, Hyderabad, pp. 120-121.
3. Gopal, Priyamvada. *The Indian English Novel: Nation, History and Narration.* Oxford: Oxford University Press, 2009. Print.

least a million were killed in retaliatory violence undertaken by members of all three communities while thousands of women were abducted, raped, and in many instances, forced to commit suicide to preserve the 'honour' of their communities. Suddenly, religious identity seemed to take precedence over all other ways of being and relating to each other.

The horrific carnage and trauma of Partition seemed to stun the intelligentsia into a stupor, but very little writing about partition came out.

Josna Rege avers,[1] Some writers attempted to relive the trauma and violence through personal memory but could account for the Partition only in terms of sin and madness. One of the notable voices at that time was inevitably that of Manto, a master teller. M.Asaduddin points out,[2] "The areas of human experience and the liminal spaces that he focused on relentlessly, shocked people out of their complacency into a new awareness of reality around them. This is particularly true in the context of his writings about the partition of India".

The poignancy of his stories on Partition transcends boundaries, the characters he invented like Toba Tek Singh or Ram Khilavan remain etched in readers' minds to an extent that Manto gets identified with these characters. Aatish Taseer in his book where he attempts Manto's translations underlines this fact that while most writers of fiction covertly include details from their lives, Manto goes further, and in many stories he included an eponymous Manto character–a character that corresponds to the actual men and like Maupassant whom he read and admired, wrote about a wide range of issues apart from partition.

Regarding repertoire and prose style of Manto, Khalid Hasan in his translation on Manto avers,[3]

1. Rege. Josna, Colonial Karma: Self, Action and Nation in the Indian English Novel. New York: Palgrave, 2004. Print
2. Asaduddin. M. **Introduction**. *Black Margins*. By Saadat Hasan Manto. New Delhi: Katha, 2003. p. 53.
3. Hasan, Khalid. **Introduction**, *Sadat* Hasan Manto. Partition Sketches and Stories, translated from Urdu, pp. xii.

If Manto is indeed the first representative of the contemporary Indian genre, then it might also consider how his prose includes literary devices that we now characterise as post-modern. Many of these stories feature narrative irruptions and self-reflexive commentary; he also obfuscates the clean genre limits of biography and fiction.

Aatish Taseer while referring to challenges involved in translating Manto avers,[1] "What is rich, fluent prose in Urdu can appear florid in English; Manto leaves loose ends, his sentences can be mangled". The employment of tricks and surprise endings reminds him of Maupassant's stories as pointed out by editor David Coward in his Introduction. He says,[2]

> For the short story, while admitted to be extremely difficult to manage successfully, has long been regarded as somehow second rate, not least because it is generally felt to suffer from Cleverness. Perhaps it requires too much control, so that the reader feels manipulated, and because many short stories depend so much upon irony or sudden reversals, they may seem over contrived—......

The insightful truth of life that he portrayed is most accurately expressed in his own words, as endorsed in the Introduction to his controversial work on Partition, "Black Margins",[3] He said, "If you are not familiar with the age in which we live, read my stories. If you cannot endure my stories, it means this age is unbearable".

Such truths about the world he said with immense simplicity and precision These words very succinctly describe the transgression and the silence his stories envisage, especially his Partition stories. His short stories bear ample testimony to the fact as he is the most widely read and ironically, the most controversial ones among the Urdu writings.

---

1. Taseer, Aatish. **Introduction**, *Manto. Selected Short Stories*, Vintage Penguin Random House India, 2012, pp. xxix.
2. *Ibid*, pp. xxix.
3. Asaduddin, M. Introduction. Black Margins. By Saadat Hasan Manto. New Delhi: Katha, 2003. Pp. 53.

Born in the pre-independent India Manto witnessed the gory violence of the 1919 massacre and the succeeding even far more violent cataclysm of hatred, anger and bloodshed in the years that followed partition, in the name of Freedom.

Manto's deep attachment to India albeit Bombay is well known to all and this too is a well-known fact that quite reluctantly Manto decided to leave Bombay. The incident that actually convinced him to migrate to Pakistan is worth mentioning as it unveils silence that the secular fabric our nation has always boasted about.

Manto was continuously getting news of rampant killings and when he received news of his uncle's killing in the communal riots, he was considerably shaken. He fictionalises this incident and creates Mumtaz who represents Manto in the story, *Saha'e*[1] the excerpt goes like this:

> Mumtaz casually said to Juggal (his old Hindu friend),
>
> I'm wondering what I would do if riots broke out in my neighbourhood!
>
> Yes, what would you do ? Mumtaz asked.
>
> I might kill you, Juggal said in all seriousness.
>
> Mumtaz fell silent, dead silent. His silence continued for nearly eight days and broke only when he suddenly announced that he was leaving for Karachi by ship, at 3.45, that very afternoon.

This passage occurs in the opening segment of the story, *Saha'e;* it, reverberates the haunting Silence embedded in the blood chilling, shocking turn of events that unravels how fragile and weak human relationships can become in such critical moments of political upheavals.

It nevertheless depicts within the story's compass that how relationships in a city can change through such violence. Another short story on Partition, *Ram Khilawan* however, gives a positive insight into humanity. This story is noteworthy for great economy

1. *Ibid,* pp. 168-169.

of style. Here too the thread of the story is the relationship between the narrator (impersonating Manto) and another character, his dhobi. While Mumtaz confronts the situation of fear and insecurity in *Saha'e*, the Hindu dhobi, Ram Khilawan, despite being poor and illiterate ignores the unpaid bills of his poor master and later when his Muslim master's wife helps his family by saving his wife's life, he repays by saving his life from the riotous mob.

His short stories, *Cold Meat* and *Open Up* bring out the silence embedded in the irrational, inhuman and blood chilling acts of human beings that indisputably gets influenced by political machinations complicit in such mindless state politics. What is most pathetic in this scenario is the fact that becomes the penultimate irony is that these murderous people may not know at times, if the enemy is Hindu or Muslim; the enemy is only the *Other.* Isher Singh, the protagonist under the spell of frenzy indiscriminately goes killing and looting, he sees a young injured girl from the enemy camp and carries her over the shoulder to satisfy his lust. But the realisation that he was going to copulate with a corpse completely freezes him. His beloved, Kulwant Kaur after knowing the story behind his changed behaviour and impotence kills him. Critics are unable to make out the reason behind her killing. This kind of ambiguity in Manto's stories compel readers to penetrate and interrogate the perils of silence: the hallmark of Manto's brilliance.

Open Up takes us to another shocking device invented by Manto where a young girl, Sakina who after getting separated from her father is so traumatised physically as well as emotionally by the continuous rape and assault that finally when she is traced by her father in a camp and when the doctor instructs people to open up for the light to enter, Sakina who is so inured by this command that she involuntarily, habitually "Opens Up" her shalwar. This story nails the final death of civilisation with a silence permeating the ghastly act perpetrated by male sex on females.

Both these stories nevertheless bring in Female Body as a contested site of conquest and assault, a determinant of collective honour. Urvashi Butalia, reputed critic on Partition Literature, points out that historians paid little or any attention to the experience of women during partition. The traumatic violence meted out to lakhs of such women demolished all sense of self, existential or social, granted to them by established patriarchal system. If they did not die a physical death, they died a psychological death.[1]

Yasmin Khan, in recent times avers,[2] "Women's bodies were made the passive witnesses to the disorder of the partition. The bodies of women were the surfaces on which texts were to be written and read–icons of the new nation".

Critics in different journals have also analyzed the silence on the marginalised. Sukhdev Sohail Singh remarks,[3] "Women were sites upon which communal politics was played. Conversion, kidnapping, rape and killing got communal colouring".

The critic underlines an important zone of silence that was never probed, no one ever thought of the injustices done to women in the filthy partition riots; women were the worst victims who silently bore the trauma of kidnapping, rape and killings in the name of communal hatred and even conversion to the other religion; it is shocking that such instances totally went unnoticed until writers like Kamla Bhasin and Urvashi Butalia undertake much later.

But it is quite laudable that Manto was able to sensitively surmise the pain inflicted on many such untold instances the women must have undergone. Manto's many such tales unmistakably reveal his empathy for the weak and marginalised. While Manto appears most acerbic in his tone in Partition stories, he is no less unforgiving and feels compelled to take up even themes like prostitution, religious superstition, adolescent anxiety. One can envision author's

1. Butalia, Urvashi. "Voices of Women", Indian Review of Books, Vol. V, No. 11, 1996, pp. 4-5.
2. Khan, Yasmin. *The Great Partition: the Making of India and Pakistan,* Penguin Viking, New Delhi, 2007, pp. 134.
3. Sohal, Sukhdev, Singh, **A Nightmare of two Cities: Amritsar and Lahore in 1947,** *Pre-Colonial and Colonial Punjab Society, Economy & Culture,* ed. By Reeta Grewal & Sheena Pall, Manohar, New Delhi, 2005, pp. 411.

unmitigated concern, even when almost half a dozen times he is tried for bringing obscenities in his stories.

His reply came simple and straight,[1] "How can I possibly disrobe a society that was already naked?" Manto just couldn't beautify what he found ugly nor did he hide what he felt should be unveiled; most importantly he didn't moralise. There is an indisputable mark in his writings of his ability to relate to the alienated since he himself was alienated from his family.

Invariably Manto is seen adopting Bombay almost as his homeland[2] an immigrant city, where no cultural knowledge can be assumed, where the landscape is often foreign and various, Manto, the fictional presence, declares his outsider's perspective and becomes a kind of guide to the new terrain. He marks out the world; the reader can put himself in his hands—his discoveries become part of the narrative.

He is compelled to leave India since like other Muslims he felt unsafe, however, he regretted his decision and it destroyed him. On his arrival at Lahore he wrote,[3] "Try as I did, I wasn't able to separate Pakistan from India and India from Pakistan. Again and again troubling questions rang in my mind: Will Pakistan's literature be separate from that of India?......." More poignantly come these questions from Manto[4] - "Now that we were free, had subjection ceased to exist? Who would be our slaves? Thousands of Hindus and Muslims were dying all around. Why were they dying?"

An eerie Silence prevails upon these and many such questions that need to be addressed and examined. Finally, reference to Toba Tek Singh, one character most fully realised by Manto became the most popular tale representing the frenzy and silence over the geographical and physical borderline to divide the two nations.

1. *Ibid*, pp. xii.
2. *Ibid*, pp. xxiii.
3. *Ibid*, pp. xxvi.
4. Sethi, Ali, "The Seer of Pakistan" *The New Yorker*. 20 August 2012. Web. 4 December 2015. <http://www.newyorker.com/online/blogs/books/2012/08/the-seer-of-pakistan.html>

Michel Foucault's views expressed for the marginalised become relevant at this juncture. Regarding Madness, Foucault said,[1] "Madness in its wild, untenable words, proclaims its own meaning; in its chimeras, it utters its secret truth". While Toba Tek Singh with his madness becomes Manto's alter ego; his madness itself poses a permanent, unanswered and unresolved question on the sanity of the wise, prudent intellectuals for bringing partition and the untold loss, mutilation and decay of human values, respect and dignity. Manto points to psychological rupture of both mind and soul of those for whom recovering from the torturous memory and nostalgia of partition and its untold woes might almost impossible.

Works Cited

Arvind Krishna Mehrotra. Delhi; Permanent Black, 2003: 168-192. Print, *Re-imagining the Nation, Postcolonial Literatures,* edited by Parama Sarkar, Orient Blackswan Private Limited, Hyderabad, pp. 120-121.

Asaduddin, M. "Introduction". *Black Margins.* By Saadat Hasan Manto. New Delhi: Katha, 2003. Pp. 53.

Brecht, Bertolt. "The Author as Producer", *Eagleton's Marxism and Literary Criticism*, Routledge, 2017, p. 67.

Butalia, Urvashi. "Voices of Women", Indian Review of Books, Vol. V, No. 11, 1996, pp. 4-5.

Gandhi, Leela, *'Novelists of the 1930s and 1940s.' An Illustrated History of Indian Literature in English,* ed Gopal, Priyamvada. *The Indian English Novel: Nation, History and Narration.* Oxford: Oxford UP, 2009. Print.

Gayatri Chakraborty Spivak. *The Politics of Deconstruction* Why *Spivak?* Routledge Critical Thinkers, London and New York, 2003, p. 4.

Hasan, Khalid. "Introduction", *Sadat* Hasan Manto. Partition Sketches and Stories, translated from Urdu, ppxii <http://www.newyorker.com/online/blogs/books/2012/08/the-seer-of-pakistan.html>

Khan, Yasmin. *The Great Partition: the Making of India and Pakistan,* Penguin Viking, New Delhi, 2007, p. 134.

Michael Foucault (2001). *Madness and Civilisation: A History of Insanity in the Age of Reason,* Psychological Press, p. 27.

Rege, Josna. Colonial Karma: Self, Action and Nation in the Indian English Novel. New York: Palgrave, 2004. Print.

1. Michael Foucault (2001). *Madness and Civilisation: A History of Insanity in the Age of Reason,* Psychological Press, p. 27.

Sohal, Sukhdev, Singh. "A Nightmare of two Cities: Amritsar, & Lahore in 1947, *Pre-Colonial and Colonial Punjab Society, Economy & Culture,* ed. By Reeta Grewal & Sheena Pall, Manohar, New Delhi, 2005, pp. 411.

Sethi, Ali. "The Seer of Pakistan" *The New Yorker*. 20 August 2012. Web. 4 December 2015. Taseer, Aatish, "Introduction", *Manto. Selected Short Stories,* Vintage Penguin Random House India, 2012, pp. xxix.